Tennessee District Heritage

An Illustrious Past Illuminates the Future

Honoring all the Great Men and Women who have led us to where we are today, and will lead us into the future until Jesus returns.

Biographical Sketches of the lives of some of the many who have helped develop the Tennessee District of the United Pentecostal Church

COVER: The cover photo by Harold Jaco contains W. M. Greer's Bible, Harold Jaco, Sr.'s Glasses, Mother Jackson's Glass Case, Mrs. Grover McDaniel's (Mrs. M.H. Hansford's mother) Lamp, Margaret Jaco's Doily, and books from Harold Jaco's Library. It is authentic history of Tennessee.

Library of Congress Control Number: 00-134392
ISBN: 0-939241-76-5
Copyright © 2000 by Tennessee District United Pentecostal Church
Printed in the United States of America

ACKNOWLDEGEMENTS

As one might guess, when it comes time for acknowledgements, it is impossible to give all the credit which is really due.

First let us acknowledge the permission granted to publish articles from books written by Mary Wallace, and published by the Pentecostal Publishing House in Hazelwood, MO. Articles on the lives of W. M. Greer, E. J. Douglas, Berthal Crossno, and J. C. Brickey were either copied in full, or information was drawn from them for details of the articles contained herein.

Secondly we thank those who took the time to make the contributions, either with information or articles to be published. The list seems endless; however we have attempted to ascribe credits at the beginning of each article.

Mary Jackson was the lifeline of the book. Had it not been for her diligent work, it could never have gone beyond a good idea. We are grateful for her tireless hours of accumulating, assembling, and organizing the information.

Many others were involved in the work, as well. Thanks to Imogene Hart for her typing, to Juanita Jaco and Carolyn Chester for their proof reading, and to Wayne Chester for his direction and contributions. Harold Jaco did the final assembly of the book.

The Tennessee District United Pentecostal Church has never been a "one-man-show". In that sense, this book has been a community project of many contributors. Thanks to everyone who has helped us preserve a sampling of the rapidly disappearing history of our work for the Lord. And may you, as the reader, be profoundly stricken with the sense of destiny for this fellowship in the overall plan of God's economy. May this history help shape our future!

CONTENTS

Preface 3

Foreword 5

Part I – Biographies of Early Pioneers in Tennessee 7

    A Brief History of the Tennessee District UPC 8
    H.G. Rodgers 16
    B.H. Hite 21
    J.C. Brickey 25
    A.D. Gurley 33

Part II - Biographies of First Officials of Tennessee District U. P. C. 40

    W.M. Greer, Superintendent 41
    E.E. McNatt, Secretary 59
    J.O. Wallace, Sunday School Director 64
    J.O. Moore, Conqueror's President 71
    J.H. Austin, Presbyter 77
    E.J. Douglas, Presbyter 84
    J.E. Ross, Presbyter 100
    J.W. Wallace, Presbyter 103
    O.W. Williams, Presbyter 106
    Clovis Turnbow, Missions Director 115
    Lela Holland, Ladies Auxiliary President 120
    Berthal Crossno, Ladies Auxiliary Secretary 127
    W.H. Cupples, Foreign Missions Director 136

Part III - Biographies of Deceased Department Leaders and some of the early Presbyters 155

    Roy Boling, Presbyter and Camp Caretaker 156
    George L. Glass, Missions Director 159
    A.N. Graves, Presbyter and Camp Caretaker 167
    M.H. Hansford, District Secretary 181
    R.G. Jackson, Presbyter 194

T. Richard Reed, Presbyter and Voice Editor	199
Gladys Robinson, Foreign Missionary	203
W.A. Singleton, Presbyter	208
W.T. Scott, Presbyter	212

Part IV - Biographies of Second and Third Superintendents
and Report of 50th Anniversary   215

L.H. Benson, Second Superintendent	216
Wayne Chester, Autobiography Third Superintendent	222
Fiftieth Anniversary by Carl McKellar	232

PREFACE

Pentecost in Tennessee had an illustrious beginning. Such ministers as B. H. Hite, H. G. Rodgers, J. C. Brickey, A. D. Gurley and others preached the Pentecostal message in the early 1900's. Some biographies have been written about their lives and ministry. But we have included them in this book because their ministry had a great impact in Tennessee. Following their ministry, Tennessee became a District in April 1949. The first officials were men of faith and wisdom. They laid a foundation for the district to build upon. It was my privilege to personally know each of these ministers whose stories are recorded in this book. It is my desire to give a brief history of them, so others can know and appreciate their work, their mission and learn a little of their lives.

L. H. Benson, second superintendent, desired to preserve the history of the district and its leaders. The work was begun a few years ago by Travis Grimsley. This book is the continuation of the work he started. In 1998, Wayne Chester, District Superintendent, and Harold Jaco, Jr., District Secretary, asked me to compile a book for this purpose.

We have included biographies and autobiographies of the first officials and some of the deceased presbyters and department leaders as well as those four mentioned above. Also included are the biography of the second superintendent and the autobiography of the present superintendent. Tennessee has had only three superintendents at this time. Most of the biographies are very brief. Some are taken from books compiled by Mary Wallace. Pentecostal Publishing House granted permission to use these.

I want to express deep gratitude to Imogene Hart who has spent many hours of word processing. With her expertise and dedication, it has made the task easier. She has been an invaluable support and help. I am also indebted to Juanita Jaco for her assistance and work. She was the source of most of the pictures taken from the historical material she has gathered. And without Harold Jaco, Jr., District Secretary, putting all the pictures and manuscripts in order, the task could not have been completed.

Grateful acknowledgement goes to those who have written of their companions or fathers; also to the ones who wrote their own stories. District Superintendent Wayne Chester has been a great support and encouragement. Finally, I owe much to the loyalty, patience, and confidence of my husband, Raymond. He has listened, encouraged, and loved me through it all.

With "An Illustrious Past – Illuminating the Future," we are reminded of the words of Henry Wadsworth Longfellow in "A Psalm of Life:"

> *Lives of great men all remind us*
> *We can make our lives sublime*
> *And departing leave behind us*
> *Footprints on the sands of time.*
> *Footprints that perhaps another*
> *Sailing o'er life's solemn main*
> *A forlorn and shipwrecked brother*
> *Seeing shall take heart again.*

Mary Jackson

FOREWORD

A wise man once said a mark of greatness for any person or group is a proper attitude toward three particular time periods. A great person will esteem the **PAST,** have a burning passion for the **PRESENT** and a telescopic vision to the **Future!**

Esteem for the **PAST** is necessary because it tells us much about the present and the future. Life is cyclic. The wisest man of all time tells us in Ecclesiastes 1:9 "The thing that hath been, it is that which shall be; and that which is done is that which shall be done and there is no new thing under the sun." Often we entertain some idea and think of it as new. We deceive ourselves, though, when we think we will be able to spawn something new without building on the foundation of the **Past**. The **Past** is the debt we owe both to the **Present** and the **Future**!

Passion for the **PRESENT** is so necessary. It keeps us alive with ideas and purpose. It overcomes the boredom of daily life's repetition. We can become "under-whelmed" with the "same old same old" until our lives become an exercise in futility! Passion for the **Present** gives us direction and purpose. It gives us goals and a driving desire to see them accomplished. We build upon the **Past** and reach into the challenge of each "today" with a profound sense of urgency. But we must *build upon the foundation of the PAST!*

Vision for the **FUTURE** helps us evaluate the progress of the **Present**. The destiny of tomorrow rests wholly upon the foundation of the **PAST** and blossoms from passion for the **PRESENT!** If we cut either of those cords, like an untethered blimp, the future will float aimlessly into chaos!

We cannot divorce ourselves from the **PAST** without destroying our heritage, our civilization and our culture!

Likewise, our faith has to have an historical basis. We must "...remember the works of the Lord..." Psalms 143:5. David said in Psalm 137:6, "If I do not remember thee, let my tongue cleave to the roof of my mouth." Without an appreciation and understanding of the **Past**, we might feel the Lord chose us because of our prowess and ability. Instead, we come to understand that we are in a long line of progression of God's blessings upon those whose hearts are turned toward Him.

We have tried, in the following pages, to bring to mind those whose lives have contributed greatly to the development of our Tennessee District over the years. We have tried to remember the preachers, the preaching, and the sovereign moves of the Lord, which have punctuated their passion for their **Present** with revival, profound miracles and signs and wonders.

This book evolved from the dream of Rev. L. H. Benson, to preserve our Tennessee History! Special thanks to those who have worked long and hard to bring this to pass. Mary Jackson, Travis Grimsley, Juanita Jaco, Imogene Hart, and so many others have helped make this possible. The Tennessee District owes a profound debt of gratitude, both to the great men and women whose lives inspired this book and those who made it their passion to chronicle these brief biographical sketches into a Book of Remembrance. As David said, we will "remember his marvelous works that he hath done." Psalms 105:5

Harold Jaco, Jr.
District Secretary

Brief History and Biographies of Early Pioneers in Tennessee

A BRIEF HISTORY OF THE TENNESSEE DISTRICT OF THE UNITED PENTECOSTAL CHURCH

Pentecost came early to Tennessee in the nineteen hundreds. Rev. H. G. Rodgers, a pioneer of Pentecost, came to Jackson with his family around 1911. In 1915, Rev. B. H. Hite came from the Nashville area to Bemis and began preaching in homes.

Brother Rodgers bought a lot in Jackson and a church was erected in 1914. From his meetings came such men as Brothers E. J. Douglas, J. C. Brickey, G. H. Brown, C. M. Goff, J. E. Ross, and others. Brother J. C. Brickey married Ethel Rodgers, daughter of H. G. Rodgers. They both ministered in preaching and singing in the Jackson area and other parts of the country.

These ministers won others to the Lord and they became great preachers of the gospel. Among these was Brother A. D. Gurley who married Mickey Rodgers, one of Brother Rodgers daughters. Another of his daughters, Carrie, married Brother G. H. Brown who later was District Superintendent of Arkansas. Brother Gurley became one of the foremost leaders of the Pentecostal Church, Inc. He was for many years Superintendent of the Southeastern District.

In 1945, the Pentecostal Church, Inc. and the Pentecostal Assemblies of Jesus Christ merged into the United Pentecostal Church, Inc. At that time, Brother Gurley was made Superintendent of the Southern District which included Tennessee, Alabama, and Mississippi.

In 1949, at a Conference of the Southern District at the Bemis Pentecostal Church, this district was divided into three districts: Tennessee, Alabama, and Mississippi. Brother W. M. Greer, pastor of Bemis Pentecostal Church, was elected Superintendent of the new Tennessee District. He served in this office for twenty-nine years.

In the same year, leaders were appointed or elected to head each department. The first District Secretary was Brother E. E. McNatt. Brother J. O. Wallace was Sunday school Director; Brother J. O. Moore was Conquerors President. Five Presbyters were elected at this Conference. They were: Brothers J. W. Wallace, E. J. Ross, O. W. Williams, J. H. Austin, and E. J. Douglas. In 1951, the District was divided into three Sections: Western, Middle, and Eastern. Presbyters for the Western Section were Brothers O. W. Williams and J. H. Austin. In the Middle Section were Brothers E. J. Douglas and R. G. Jackson. Brothers J. W. Wallace and W. T. Scott served the Eastern Section.

The desire to build new churches in Tennessee caused the district officials to form the Missions Department in 1953. Brother Clovis Turnbow was the first director of this department.

Camp Meetings had been a great part of the Southern District. Land had been purchased near Iuka, Mississippi and for a few years meetings were held there. Then it was moved to Tupelo, Mississippi on the campus of the Bible School. When the District was divided, Brother Greer felt the need for a camp in Tennessee. In 1950, land was purchased at Perryville, Tennessee for a campground. The first Camp Meeting was held in August 1951. Rev. and Mrs. Norman Paslay were the Evangelists. The great meetings held there by the youth, District Conferences and Camp Meetings are a thrilling part of the history of the Tennessee District. Truly, the Camp Ground was often referred to, "Holiness Hill" and the "Heart Throb" of the District. With the camp meetings and other needs on the campground, Brother Greer realized the ladies of the District should be organized. In 1954, the Ladies Auxiliary was set in order with Sister Lela Holland as president and Sister Berthal Crossno as secretary. This department proved to be a wonderful blessing to the District.

In 1962, Brother W. M. Greer resigned as pastor of the Bemis Pentecostal Church to become full-time District Superintendent. He had pastored the church for over twenty-one years. The records show a remarkable growth in the district after this step of faith by Brother Greer.

The campground consisted of the big tabernacle, dining hall, kitchen, lunch stand and a few dormitories. Different churches built cabins for their congregations to occupy during camp meetings and other meetings. A beautiful girl's dormitory was built in 1968. The Ladies Auxiliary built a lovely Ladies Lounge in 1969. The same year the old rustic appearance of camp buildings gave way to more modern structures. The tabernacle was completely renovated. Adding to the convenience and beauty of the grounds a new all steel assembly building was constructed.

Many wonderful services were enjoyed in the following years in these facilities. Youth Camps grew until it was necessary to have two camps. The Junior Camp, under the direction of the Sunday School Department, saw many juniors repent and filled with the Holy Ghost. The Senior Youth Camps were directed by the Conquerors Department.

Memories still linger of these camps. Young people who attended them still tell their children of the wonderful times they enjoyed at Youth Camp on "Holiness Hill."

Property was purchased in Jackson, Tennessee at 31 Harts Bridge Road in 1972 for a District Office. The building was completed and occupied in early 1973. This had been a dream of Brother Greer for many years - to have a District Office for the superintendent, secretary and office secretary. Prior to this new office, the district's secretarial work had been done in the church office of Brother M. H. Hansford. Brother Hansford was elected to serve in this office in 1959 and served until his retirement in 1980. He was pastoring a church in Memphis, and Lorene Beaty assisted him as office secretary. When he was elected pastor of the Lexington Avenue Church in Jackson, he moved the secretarial work to this office and Mary Jackson was office secretary. Mary had been assisting Brother Greer in the District work in his office at the Bemis Church. A step to reach Brother Greer's dream was the move to a small house on Morton Street in Bemis. This office was occupied by Brother Greer, Brother Hansford and Mary Jackson. Mary resigned as office secretary in 1972 to work full time at the Bemis Post Office, and Joan Holland filled the position of office secretary for a few months. She was followed by Alice Grisham. So it was the wonderful privilege of Brother Greer, Brother Hansford and Alice Grisham to move into the grand new office at 31 Harts Bridge Road.

During Brother Greer's tenure, the District grew from 24 churches to over 100 churches. The assets of the District increased from a very few dollars to a well-developed campground which could conservatively be valued at $300,000. Also, the new District Office was paid in full. He resigned in the middle of his fifteenth two-year term in 1978 due to the failing health of Sister Greer. He had served 29 years as Superintendent. The District was completely debt-free and with several thousand dollars in the bank.

Brother L. H. Benson was elected to complete the unfinished term of Brother Greer as District Superintendent. He was elected at the next District Conference in April 1979. He held this office until he retired in April 1995.

While Brother Benson was Superintendent, the camp meetings continued at Perryville until 1987. Because the old tabernacle was not large enough to hold the crowds and inadequate in every way, the camp meeting was held in Jackson, Tennessee at the Civic Center beginning in July 1988. The Camp ground at Perryville was still used for youth camps until it was sold in 1993. The youth camps were held at Garner Creek Camp beginning in 1994 until 1999.

In October 1993, the old Camp Ground at Perryville was sold. Brother Benson and Brother Wayne Chester, District Secretary, recommended a committee with the District Board to select a new site in Middle Tennessee at Bon Aqua. Plans for purchasing began in July 1994 and the deal was closed September 6 of the same year. This new campground was given the name "Lake Benson Camp and Christian Retreat Center."

In 1994, Brother Benson and the District Board felt it good to have the camp meeting at Nashville, Tennessee. This would make it easier for the churches in that area and in East Tennessee to attend. It returned to Jackson Civic Center in 1995.

Under the leadership of Brother Benson as Superintendent, one hundred new ministers were licensed and twenty-two new churches were added to the district. A program known as "Build a Church in a Day" was begun to help Home Missions. This proved successful and two churches were built. One was built at Sevierville and another at Dayton.

Brother Benson retired in April 1995 and Brother Wayne Chester was elected District Superintendent. Brother Harold Jaco was elected to the office of District Secretary which was vacated by Brother Chester becoming Superintendent.

On the shoulders of Brother Chester fell, not only the care of all the churches but also the responsibility to build Lake Benson Camp Ground. Workdays were scheduled by different Sections of the District and many brethren began to give of their time to get work done on the Camp.

The theme Brother Chester chose for his work as Superintendent was "Do it for the Children." With this vision work began in earnest to complete Lake Benson. The first phase was a lounge. This could serve as a place for the workers to reside who were working at the camp. Work also began on the dining hall, kitchen and two dormitories. In order to have the youth camp on the grounds in the year 2000, a large multi-purpose building was constructed.

One project to raise funds for the new campground was selling bricks for a memorial to be built in memory of Brother W. M. Greer, first District Superintendent. This monument will be erected near the lounge and dining hall.

The Tennessee District has grown from twenty-four churches to one hundred forty-three as of January 2000. There are three hundred twenty-five ministers licensed to work in the district as pastors, evangelists, teachers, and assistants. God has greatly blessed the Tennessee District with the leadership of three great men - Brother W. M. Greer, Brother L. H. Benson and Brother Wayne Chester. These were and are men of integrity, men who were honest, sincere, and full of wisdom and faith, men who gave of their time, talent and labor to make Tennessee one of the great districts of the United Pentecostal Church. Ours is a district with a heritage we can be thankful and happy to pass to our children and the following generations.

To God be the Glory!

Mary Jackson

C.M. Goff, A.N. Graves, Novel Fry, Gov. Frank Clement, E.E. McNatt, W.M. Greer, and O. W. Williams

Rev. & Mrs. Norman Pasley and Young Norman singing at Tennessee District Camp Meeting at Perryville, TN

The Old Dining Hall at Perryville Camp Ground

Tennessee District Heritage 15

An early Tennessee District Board: (standing) O.W. Williams, R.G. Jackson, J. W. Wallace, E.E. McNatt, W.T. Scott; (seated) J.H. Austin, J. O. Moore, E. J. Douglas, W.M. Greer.

A Dream Come True: The new District Office was ready to occupy in 1973.

HENRY GREEN RODGERS
By Mary Brickey Rogers

The year was 1864, and Perry County in Tennessee was feeling the effects of the Civil War. Family life on the farm was not easy, yet it was during this year that Henry Green Rodgers was born – a baby whose life was to reach into an unstable world and cause many souls to change their destiny.

In 1886, Henry met a young lady by the name of Emma Jenny LaRue. Jenny had grown up on a farm in the same county. Even though she was only sixteen years old, after a short courtship, they were married that same year.

After his conversion, Henry received the light on healing, and God healed his baby girl, Ethel, who had not been expected to live. In 1903, God called Henry to preach. Six years later when he and Jenny heard the truth of the baptism of the Holy Ghost, they sought and soon received this experience.

During those difficult early years of her marriage, Sister Rodgers gave birth to ten children; however, only four of them lived. Sister Rodgers and the children traveled with Brother Rodgers over Alabama and neighboring states, hoping each brief stop would be the final destination. While living in Montgomery, Alabama, their eleventh child, a baby girl named Evelyn was born in October of 1911. Sister Rodgers kept hoping they would finally settle down in one place, but they continued traveling. "Oh, just as soon as we get settled, we have to move again," she cried.

On his evangelistic tours, Brother Rodgers was often accompanied by his daughter, Ethel, who started preaching on street corners and in jail services when she was only nine years old. When God spoke to Brother Rodgers to go to Jackson, Tennessee, in late February of 1912, he and Ethel, who was seventeen at this time, left for that city. He rented a room for his daughter, while he slept on the benches in Union Station Depot -- that is until they ran him off.

In search for a house for his family, Brother Rodgers met a man by the name of Hicks, whose heart the Lord had moved upon to rent Brother Rodgers a house. Mr. Hicks accepted the agreement that Brother Rodgers would have no rent payment for the first three months. Finally, in December of 1912, he sent for his family, informing Sister Rodgers to roll up double blankets and bring them as carry-on baggage on the train.

Sister Rodgers and the four younger children arrived at midnight. With no means of transportation, they had to walk three or four miles to get to their new home. The blankets they had carried aboard the train were laid on hay that Brother Rodgers had gathered for their beds. They had no money to get their baggage from the depot, but the Lord moved upon the heart of a black minister to give them $18.00. This was enough to get their baggage and their furniture out. For the first six weeks, the family survived by eating mush and milk for every meal. The realtor, Mr. Hicks, gave them a cow, with no payment expected -- just an agreement to provide the cow's feed.

During this time, Brother Rodgers conducted street meetings and erected a tent. He was assisted in the meetings by his daughter, Ethel. She played the piano, sang and preached. They preached a message of Holy Ghost baptism and a life of holiness; they had not yet received the revelation of baptism in Jesus' name. In 1912, a lot was bought and a church was erected in 1914. This was to become the "mother" church of the baptism in the name of the Lord Jesus in that area.

Brother Rodgers attended a conference in 1914 in Hot Springs, Arkansas, held by the General Council of the Assemblies of God. Baptism in the name of Jesus Christ was discussed. Brother Rodgers left the conference stirred in his soul, and in the summer of 1915, he was the host pastor in Jackson to the Third Interstate Encampment of the Assemblies of God. At this camp, Brother E. N. Bell and Brother Rodgers discussed the truth of baptism in the name of Jesus Christ. Then they requested Brother L. V. Roberts of Indianapolis, Indiana to come and preach for them. Brother Roberts had been baptized in the name of the Lord Jesus Christ by Brother Glenn Cook in Indianapolis on March 6, 1915,

Brother Roberts preached the truth of baptism in the name of the Lord Jesus. At the close of Brother Roberts' sermon, Brother Bell and Rro. Rodgers were baptized in the name of the Lord Jesus in the Forked Deer River. The following day, 56 believers were baptized in the wonderful name of the Lord Jesus. Rev . E. J. Douglas and his wife were baptized along with many others who had been converted in the meetings.

The first convert in these meetings in Jackson was a young man by the name of J. C. Brickey. In 1913, Brother Brickey married Brother Rodgers' daughter, Ethel. They entered the gospel work, Ethel doing the preaching and Brother Brickey leading the singing. He had a wonderful voice and God honored the songs he sang for Him. He and

Ethel evangelized middle and west Tennessee, northern Mississippi, and southern Illinois. They pastored the Jackson church at intervals. Brother Brickey was pastoring the Jackson church when he died in 1939. Ethel died in 1954.

Two other daughters of H. G. and Emma Jenny LaRue Rodgers also married into the ministry. In June 1922, Carrie married G. Hobert Brown, who was later called into the ministry and pastored the church in Little Rock, Arkansas for 41 years until his death in 1965. Brother Brown was also Superintendent of the Arkansas District for several years. After Brother Brown's death, his wife, Sister Carrie, bought a home in Jackson, Tennessee where she lived until her death in 1991.

Mickey Rodgers was married to A. D. Gurley in June of 1923. Brother Gurley was well known in the Pentecostal ranks. He served as pastor of Bemis Pentecostal Church, and later pastored at Corinth, Mississippi for 46 years before his retirement. Mickey died in 1974, and Brother Gurley died in 1976.

The only son who grew to manhood, is also buried in Jackson, Tennessee. The baby girl, Evelyn, passed away in 1978 and is buried in Florida.

After founding the church in Jackson, Brother and Sister Rodgers, with their family, moved to Stuttgart, Arkansas, where he started a work. The remaining years of their lives were spent working for God in Arkansas, northern Mississippi, and in Picton, Ontario, Canada.

In 1938 they moved to Hohenwald, Tennessee. Six months before Sister Rodgers passed away, they moved to Nashville, Tennessee to the home of their youngest daughter Evelyn. In 1940, at the age of 71 Sister Rodgers went home to be with the Lord. She was buried in Dyer,

Tennessee. Brother Rodgers lived to be 86 years of age and died in 1950.

The influence of Jenny and Henry Rodgers and this dedicated family has touched lives and brought truth to many souls. Ethel Rodgers Brickey, in memory of her mother wrote the following eulogy.

SUNRISE OVER DYER CEMETERY

Oh! Glory of the immortal!

Then we will behold the scars of those who battled so bravely. The warriors and pilgrims will shine as the noonday sun.

My mother, who fought such glorious battles; who shared in conflict against the forces of darkness; whose heart ached and many tears shed; whose prayers still linger in the minds and memories of her children; whose hands ministered and served, washed and scrubbed, that her children might have food and necessities; she will stand more glorious than the queens of the earth. Her treasures were few here, for she locked them all in the vault of heaven, where moths do not corrupt nor thieves steal.

B. H. HITE
By Mary Jackson

Benjamin Harrison Hite was born September 2, 1888 in Franklin, Kentucky. One of seven children born to John and Emily Hite, he was destined to have a great part in the work of God.

His mother was laid to rest when he was only ten years of age. At her passing, she made a profound impression upon her young son by saying that she would not mind dying if she knew that he and his younger sister would grow up to serve the Lord.

Upon reaching adulthood, B. H. Hite moved from Franklin, Kentucky to Nashville, Tennessee where he became employed in the Leather Shop of the Tennessee State Prison. He was united in marriage with Mary Vanover on December 26, 1911 in Nashville. To this union was born ten children.

In 1912, when he was still a young man, God began to deal with B. H. Hite. He was converted in a cottage prayer meeting. At this time, he wholly accepted God as his healer and threw away all his medicine. A few days later, H. W. Coulon came to Nashville, preaching the message of the baptism of the Holy Ghost. B. H. Hite had never heard this message, but when he did, he said that he wanted all God had for him. In October 1912, he received the Holy Ghost at a ladies prayer meeting and spoke with tongues for about five or six hours. Shortly thereafter he acknowledged his call to preach the gospel.

At the beginning of his ministry, he preached on street corners, in jails, in cottage prayer meetings – in fact, anywhere there was an open door. In his first cottage prayer meeting, a blind woman was divinely healed. Surely this was, in a sense, prophetic of his future ministry, for many were divinely healed through the years as he prayed for them. He opened his first mission in 1913 somewhere in the Johnson Street vicinity. The theme of B. H. Hite's ministry was St. Mark's statement: "These signs shall follow them that believe." Many notable miracles occurred. In the service where the blind woman was healed, a group of youth from Treveca College who had come to help in the service, became frightened and left when she was instantly healed.

He soon felt the call to enter evangelistic work, and this led him into mountain areas, as well as to many places in Tennessee, Arkansas, Oklahoma, Illinois and Missouri. He founded missions that have grown into fine churches. He left the Middle Tennessee area and came to the Bemis area in 1915. Here he preached in homes. Among the first to receive the Holy Ghost was Ernest Shindoll, who later became a Pentecostal minister. The A. G. Webb home was one place Brother Hite preached. Mother Webb once said that Brother Hite only had three messages: one on the Holy Ghost, one on healing, and one on the Second Coming of Christ. A tent was erected in Bemis and as the crowd grew, so did the opposition. So strong was the opposition that a Bill of Injunction was filed and the tent was moved to "Happy Hollow." Revival fires were burning! The Bemis

Pentecostal Church began with these services. Brother Hite pastored the Bemis Church for about two years.

In 1921, he went to St. Louis, Missouri to start a church. At the time he had two children. He came into the city with only three dollars. On that same day, he gave half of this to a needy fellow minister. (Such was typical of him.) He had faith that God would take care of him and God did. In St. Louis, he established the First Pentecostal Church and pastored it until his death twenty-seven years later. God mightily blessed his labors and gave him many souls. In the St. Louis area, there are today some thirty churches either directly or indirectly an outgrowth of his ministry. From his church, approximately forty ministers went out into the work of God.

B. H. Hite's first ministerial affiliation was with the Assemblies of God. Then in 1916, he received the light on baptism in Jesus Name and affiliated with the Pentecostal Assemblies of the World. Later he became a member of the Pentecostal Church, Incorporated. Brother Hite played a prominent role in helping to bring about the merger of the Pentecostal Church, Incorporated and the Pentecostal Assemblies of Jesus Christ. From the time of the merger in 1945 until his death, he was a faithful member of the United Pentecostal Church.

He served in various official positions. He was the first General Chairman of the Pentecostal Church, Incorporated, being elected in 1934 and serving until 1939. On October 22, 1937, the General Conference of the PCI opened in Jackson, Tennessee at the National Guard Armory and Brother Hite as General Chairman, was in charge and gave the opening address. He also attended a special dinner sponsored by George Smith and held at the largest and most prestigious hotel in the city. This banquet was attended by the Jackson Mayor H. B. Foust and School

Superintendent C. B. Ijams and twenty-one delegates of the Pentecostal Church, Inc. Conference. The Wednesday night service of the Conference was given to divine healing with Brother Hite in charge and many were prayed for and healed. In this same organization, he later held the position of District Superintendent of the Central District, made up at that time of Illinois, Missouri, and Kentucky. When Missouri separated from the Central District to form a district of its own, he became their District Superintendent. He continued to hold this position in the United Pentecostal Church until the time of his death.

On May 23, 1948, B. H. Hite was called home to be with the Lord. His funeral was held in St. Louis, Missouri with Brother A. D. Gurley as minister. He may be gone from this life, but the work he did lives on.

(Left) Early Photo of the B.H. Hite family.

(Right) The B. H. Hite Memorial Organ at the Bemis Pentecostal Church.

(Below) A later picture of the B.H. Hite Family.

J. C. BRICKEY
By Mary Brickey Rogers

*J*udge Chester Brickey did not grow up wanting to be a minister. That was God's idea – not his.

He was born in Jackson, Tennessee on February 12, 1890, the older of two sons born to Meredith Coleman Brickey and Mattie Jane Brickey. His parents both died when he and his brother, Elbert David, were children, and a relative took care of them.

As a young man, he became known as one of the community's ruffians, riding the rods, and carousing in the pool halls and the saloons. He had only a grammar school education, but as he grew older, he became an apprentice to the pattern maker's trade, and obtained a position as a pattern maker with Southern Engine Boiler Works, which kept him from serving in World War I.

Sometime during these years, he had a dream. He dreamed he was in a watermelon patch, stealing watermelons, when suddenly the watermelon patch sprung up with lilies. A voice spoke to him from one of the lilies and talked to him about giving his heart to God. At the time, he did not realize the significance of the dream.

One night, when he was twenty-two, he was attracted to a tent meeting, where a seventeen-year-old lady by the name of Ethel Rodgers was preaching, along with her father, Brother Henry G. Rodgers. They preached a message of repentance, giving up your old life of sin, being baptized (in the titles), and then a person would receive an infilling of the Holy Ghost, evidenced by speaking in a heavenly language.

Judge Brickey became the first convert in this meeting. Soon the community could see the transformation that had taken place in this young man's life. He had stolen a hat from McCall Hughes Men's Clothing Store, and one of the first things he did after his conversion was to confess stealing the hat to the management of McCall Hughes, and offer to make restitution.

The next year, 1913, he was married to the young lady preacher, Ethel Rodgers. Soon he felt the call of God upon his life for the ministry, and in 1914, both he and Sister Ethel were ordained by the General Council of the Assemblies of God. In this same year, they began to evangelize as the doors were opened to them.

In 1914, a lot had been purchased on 322 Lexington Avenue and a church built and set in order by the pastor, Rev. H. G. Rodgers. In the summer of 1915, Brother Rodgers was the host pastor in Jackson to the Third Interstate Encampment of the Assemblies of God. The year before, Brother Rodgers had attended a conference held by the General Council of the Assemblies of God in Hot Springs, Arkansas. Baptism in the name of the Lord Jesus was discussed. Brother Rodgers left the conference stirred in his soul.

Brother E. N. Bell was then the Chairman of the General Council of the Assemblies of God, and he and Brother Rodgers decided to invite Brother L. V. Roberts to speak to the camp. Brother Roberts had been baptized in the name of the Lord Jesus by Brother Glen Cook in

Indianapolis in March of that year. He preached the truth of baptism in Jesus' name. Although Brother Bell and Brother Rodgers knew this, they still sent Brother Roberts a telegram from the camp meeting: "We want your message for the camp; take first train." Signed: Pastor H. G. Rodgers and E. N. Bell.

Brother Roberts took the train at once. After arriving in Jackson, he began preaching Acts 2:38. As a result of his message, Brother E. N. Bell and Brother Rodgers were the first to be baptized in the name of the Lord Jesus. Another baptizing was held on Sunday afternoon. Among those baptized were J. C. and Ethel Brickey; Brother and Sister E. J. Douglas; Brother and Sister C. M. Goff; Brother J. A. Bennett; Sister H. G. Rodgers along with fifty-five others.

Since so many ministers and laymen had been baptized in the name of the Lord Jesus by 1916, the General Council of the Assemblies of God prepared a statement of fundamental beliefs which the Oneness ministers could not accept. They were forced to form a Oneness organization of their own. E. N. Bell wavered and stayed with the General Council of the Assemblies of God. In 1920, Brother Bell wrote Brother Brickey a letter stating why he could no longer baptize in the name of the Lord Jesus Christ. That letter has been given to the Historical Center, United Pentecostal Church International.

This new organization formed by the Oneness brethren was called the General Assembly of the Apostolic Assemblies. The only published ministerial list of the General Assembly of the Apostolic Assemblies contained 154 names. Among those who affiliated was Brother J. C. Brickey. But this organization was short lived. An interracial organization called the Pentecostal Assemblies of the World was formed, and in 1919 Brother and Sister

Brickey became affiliated with this organization. Their credentials were signed by E. W. Doak, General Chairman, and G. T. Haywood, General Secretary.

In the early 1920's, Brother Brickey became pastor of the Jackson church. During the years of his pastorate, several outstanding preachers ministered to the church. Among those who preached were: Brother Andrew Urshan, Brother L. C. Hall, Brother William E. Booth-Clibborn, and others. It was during his pastorate in 1925, that a conference was held in which the Pentecostal Ministerial Alliance was organized. In 1932, the P.M.A. became the Pentecostal Church, Incorporated. Brother Brickey was a General Presbyter with the P.C.I. until his death.

Brother Brickey had an unusual desire for the Word of God, and he studied constantly. It was remarkable how the Lord helped him in acquiring a knowledge of the Scriptures. He was blessed, not only to have an evangelistic ministry, but also a teaching ministry.

He became a student of prophecy, and in 1929 he constructed a huge canvas chart, which he used in some of his campaigns. The artistic work on this chart was painted by Sister Isabel Flowers of Pinckneyville, Illinois. Later, he had an engraving made for smaller, individual charts, which he printed and sold in his meeting when he taught on prophecy.

He held many successful campaigns in different parts of the country, especially in middle and western Tennessee. Many people were baptized in Jesus' name and filled with the Holy Ghost in these revivals. Many summers the family would be gone from home as soon as school was out for summer vacation, until school started in the fall.

Sister Berthal Crossno gives an account of a meeting held in Benton County, Tennessee. "Brother J. C. Brickey came to Benton County along with Brother C. M. Goff about 1922. They preached out in the country, south of Camden. One of my older brothers, along with some of his buddies went. They had never heard such singing and preaching. When Willie told my dad and mother, they told him he had better stay away because the preachers would put some kind of powder on him.

"In July of 1924 Brother and Sister Brickey pitched a tent at the old depot in south Camden. They preached for two weeks. The crowds came. At the same time, Brother Goff was preaching a revival near Chalk Level. They had a joint baptizing and Brother and Sister Cain were baptized.

"In the following September they came back again with the tent. I was thirteen years old, at that time, and I told my parents I wanted to be baptized. They agreed. I was afraid of the water, and Brother Brickey sensed it. He told me I could kneel down closer to the edge. When he laid me back in the lovely name of Jesus, as the water rolled over my head, the sweetest peace flooded my soul. Fears went away! I received the Holy Ghost later, but my experience of water baptism I have cherished through the years. At the conferences in later years, I always was thrilled with the dynamic preaching of Brother Brickey, and his unique way of delivery."

After evangelizing in southern Illinois during the summer of 1928, Brother Brickey accepted the pastorate of the church in Pinckneyville, Illinois, which he pastored until August, 1929. He became pastor of the Bryan Avenue church in Granite City, Illinois and stayed at this church until November 1930, when they moved back to Jackson, Tennessee.

Brother Brickey had a beautiful singing voice, and God honored the songs that he sang for Him. (His only son, James, inherited his beautiful voice.) Among some of the favorites which Brother Brickey sang in his meetings and at

General Conferences were: "Across the Great Divide," "His Eye Is On the Sparrow," "God's Tomorrow," and "Shall I Empty Handed Be?"

He composed a song, "O, 'Twas Jesus," copyrighted in 1930. It was published in an early edition of *Pentecostal Praises*. It was his personal testimony.

As a sheep I had wandered far away from the fold,
And the face of the shepherd I could not behold.
Out on sin's dark mountain I was wounded and cold.
But the voice of the shepherd called me back to the fold.
I was lost in the darkness and in sin's dreary night,
But my blessed Redeemer came and brought me the light.
Now the peace of Jesus, O, it shines so bright!
By His life-giving presence, He has ended the night.

CHORUS: *O, 'twas Jesus; O, 'twas Jesus;*
         O, 'twas Jesus saved my sinful soul.
         O, 'twas Jesus; O, 'twas Jesus;
         O, 'twas Jesus made the wounded whole.

Now I walk with the Saviour with my face to the light
And the sunbeams of heaven make my pathway bright.
And some day He will call me from this world of strife,
And will crown me with glory and eternal life.

Like Paul of old, Brother Brickey became a tentmaker. While pastoring the Bryan Avenue church in Granite City, Illinois, he bought a tent machine. With the help of his oldest daughter, Mary, and his son, James, he made three gospel tents. After moving back to Tennessee in November of 1930, they continued to make gospel tents.

In the summer of 1939, although Brother Brickey was ill with a heart condition, they made a tent for the church in

Bemis, Tennessee. In July, when it was completed and erected, Brother Brickey prayed the dedicatory prayer on a Saturday night. God blessed him in an unusual way. The following Saturday morning, July 8, 1939, he was called from this world of strife, and crowned with glory and eternal life, as his song had said.

At the time of his death, he was pastor of the church in Jackson, which position he had occupied at different intervals for more than ten years. He was forty-nine years of age, and was survived by his wife, Sister Ethel, one son, James, and three daughters, Mary, Naoma, and Genevieve.

Ethel Rodgers, 1913.

Bro. & Sis. Brickey at Napier, Tennessee

The Brickey's after Bro. Brickey's death in 1941: Mary, Naoma, James, Genevive and Sis. Brickey

ALBERT DEWY GURLEY
By Travis Grimsley

Pentecost, as many of us know it today, began with a man named A. D. Gurley.

Albert Dewy Gurley was born in Decatur County, Tennessee on August 25, 1889. He was the second son of Mr. and Mrs. A. J. Gurley. From early childhood, he had a tendency toward spiritual things. At the age of nine years, in desperation, he prayed his first earnest prayer, and God answered it as realistically as any prayer He would ever answer for him. When just a lad of thirteen years, working in the corn field, he was gripped with such a hunger for God that he knelt between the rows of corn and fully surrendered his heart to the Lord.

Even though his father had him sprinkled at an early age, he felt now the need to be baptized by immersion. So his father took him to Lexington, Tennessee where Fleetwood Hall, a Baptist minister immersed him in the Name of the Father and of the Son and of the Holy Ghost.

In the year 1916, two preachers by the names of E. J. Douglas and J. C. Bricky, with their singers and musicians came to Parsons, Tennessee preaching something new and different. Albert Gurley was among those who attended those services. He had never heard such "anointed" preaching and singing. He was so fascinated by it that he, along with his sister – after a hard day's work in the fields – would practically run the three miles to the services. They did not want to miss a word of a song. These people were preaching something about being "baptized in Jesus Name" and about receiving the "Holy Ghost" and speaking with "other tongues!" After about three weeks without a move being made by anyone, to his sorrow and disappointment, the meeting came to a close. Had this been real or fantasy? He wondered.

However, the seed had been sown, and it had fallen on good ground. One year later, to his joy, the evangelistic team returned. Meanwhile, Albert Gurley had not been idle. He had read and searched his Bible and was now convinced that what he had heard preached a year before was the TRUTH. He was the first one in his family, the first one in the town of Parsons, Tennessee to accept this truth and be baptized in the Name of Jesus. It was in a brush arbor meeting at Mt. Tabor, Tennessee on July 30, 1918 that Albert Gurley received the marvelous gift of the Holy Ghost.

At this time, the United States was engaged in World War I, and he, along with many other young men, was called on to fulfill his obligation to his country. However, the day before his induction into the armed services, the armistice was signed, and he was excused from military service.

He then went to Muscle Shoals, Alabama to work. Although the influenza epidemic of 1918 was rampant, God protected and spared him for the great work he was to do.

About November 21, 1918, he went to a Pentecostal service and during a testimony service, he stood and testified. After he was seated, Brother Berry, the minister, announced, "Next Sunday, young Brother Gurley will be preaching here." Brother Gurley was shocked at the announcement and tried to explain that he was not a preacher. But Brother Berry only said, "You will be after next Sunday." So on November 28, 1918, Brother Gurley preached his first sermon. His subject was "Divine Healing." This launched the beginning of his fifty years of loyal, dedicated service to his Master.

Doors began to be opened to him. Many times he went alone, preaching, playing his guitar, singing as only he could. He also worked in large revival campaigns with other ministers, such as Brother E. J. Douglas, Brother J. C. Bricky, Brother Pitts Graves, and others. One to be especially remembered is the eleven-week revival crusade with Brother William E. Booth Clibborn in Jackson, Tennessee.

On June 16, 1923, a partner was added to the A. D. Gurley evangelistic party, when he married Miss Mickey Rodgers at Jackson, Tennessee. Preaching the gospel was nothing new to his bride, as her father, the Rev. H. G. Rodgers, was one of the pioneer ministers in Pentecost. She was not only a beautiful young lady, but was very talented as well. With her piano playing and singing, together they began to rapidly spread the good news of the gospel.

On January 2, 1924, Brother and Sister Gurley moved to Bemis, Tennessee and took the pastorate of the church there. In the year of 1926, Brother Gurley and his family were on their way to California, when God definitely spoke to him at Little Rock, Arkansas, and told him to go to Corinth, Mississippi. So in June of that year he, along with his father-in-law, Brother Rodgers, went to Corinth for the first Pentecostal revival in that city. For nine years, Brother Gurley pastored both the Bemis, Tennessee and the Corinth, Mississippi churches, preaching in Corinth on

Sunday morning and in Bemis on Sunday nights. Part of the time, he commuted by train, but many times by automobile, with his family, over fifty miles of rough gravel road, a two and one-half hour trip. Also, many Sunday afternoons, he would preach at Pleasant Hill, Mississippi, seven miles west of Corinth, before returning to Bemis for the night services. It was there at Pleasant Hill that he preached, carrying a letter in his pocket which threatened his life if he continued to preach this gospel there. Of course, that did not stop him, and today a beautiful church stand there as a monument to the fruits of his labor, along with the saints of that congregation.

Although times were hard in 1929, at the beginning of the depression, Brother Gurley and his congregation at Bemis, Tennessee, erected a new church building to the glory of God and the saving of many souls.

It was in the year 1935 that Brother Gurley decided to move his family to Corinth to plan and supervise an addition to the church on Tate Street. In that year, he brought in the Booneville, Mississippi church. The family moved back to Bemis, Tennessee for the year 1936, but in 1937 they moved back to Corinth into the beautiful parsonage that the people had erected on North Jackson Street.

Brother and Sister Gurley were blessed with six children, two sons and four daughters. Like their parents, they were all talented in music, and their parents developed this talent by intensive training during their younger years. They became a great help to their parents in the ministry of the gospel.

Brother Gurley with his three oldest children, Rentz, Doris, and Joe, and with Sis Gurley at the piano, formed the famous "Gurley Family Quartet." This quartet went far and near singing for the glory of God and preaching the Word.

Those who remember hearing them will never forget how they blessed the people with their singing. Many of the songs they sung were composed, both words and music, by Brother Gurley as he was not only a preacher, but a song writer as well.

Along with the many joys of life, there comes the sadness and sorrows. During World War II on October 25, 1944, in battle with the Japanese fleet off Samar Island near Leyte Gulf, their oldest son, Thomas Rentz, lost his life in the service of this country. It was in the months to follow that they found Luke 4:18 to be real, that Jesus not only came to save and to heal, but also to bind up the brokenhearted.

After the four older children were about grown, they were blessed with two daughters, Demmy and Donna, who were such a blessing with all their talent in music and singing.

For 22 years, along with pastoring two churches and holding revivals, Brother Gurley held the position of District Superintendent. In 1950, he was elected to the Foreign Missionary Board, where he worked faithfully.

Brother Gurley preached approximately 15,000 sermons and baptized more that 2,000 persons. From this fifty years of fruitful ministry has come at least 39 preachers to help perpetuate this gospel. One of these was called to the Foreign Missions Field and served three terms in West Africa.

On September 5, 1976, Brother Gurley passed from this life to be with his Lord. Funeral services were held on Tuesday, September 7 at the First Pentecostal Church in Corinth, Mississippi, a church he founded and pastored for many years. Speaker for the service was Rev. Marvin H. Hansford, secretary of the Tennessee District. He gave a brief history of Brother Gurley's life and spoke from the text in II Samuel 3:38. Others speaking in the service were Brother Cecil Bennett, Brother Lee J. Edwards, Brother Stanley W. Chambers, Brother Nathaniel Urshan and Brother W. M. Greer. The local newspaper in Corinth said of him, "Rev. A. D. Gurley spent most of his life helping to shoulder other people's problems and teaching them to face their responsibilities. He was called 'a great man,' 'a soul winner,' 'an evangelist,' and a 'leader.' But to many of his Pentecostal colleagues, he was a 'prince among preachers.' He was a preacher's preacher. For 54 years he preached the gospel wherever people would listen. Tuesday they held the funeral for Brother Gurley. It was, of course a sad day ..."

Brother Gurley was preceded in death by his wife, Sis. Mickey Gurley in 1974.

If it could ever truthfully be said of any man that he "served his generation well," it surely could be said of Brother A. D. Gurley.

(Above) A. D. Gurley, M. H. Hansford, and Howard A. Goss.

(Right) The Gurley Family: A.D., Mickey, Doris, Rentz, Ruth, and Joe.

Tennessee District Heritage 39

The traditional A.D. Gurley friendliness: from the front steps, on the street, or at the front door of the church, it was always the same. The Family gathered to wish someone a happy trip on their way here.

A. D. Gurley preached with great power and anointing. Many thousands were baptized and filled with the Holy Ghost under his ministry!

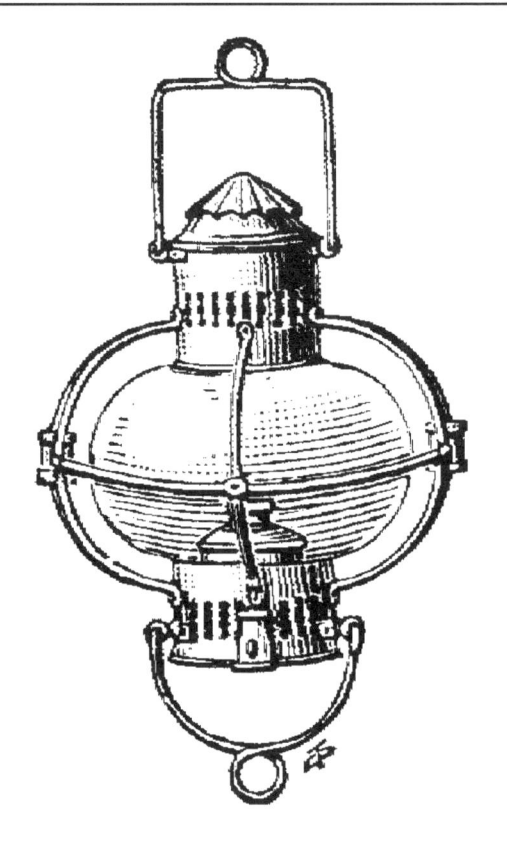

Biographies of the First Officials of the Tennessee District U. P. C.

WILLIS McCLELLAN GREER
By Ann Brinkley Luther

On the warm summer day of August 11, 1906, Willis McClellan Greer was born in a one-room log cabin in Benton County, Tennessee, near the small town of Camden. Unknown to anyone at that time, this infant was born in an area that was destined in just a few short years to become the cradle of Oneness Pentecost for that area of the United States.

Willis McClellan was the fourth of seven children born to Jim Willie Greer and Elizabeth McEwen Greer. The other children were Maude, Vivian, Allie, William, who died at the age of nine, Earnestine, who died at the age of three, and Truman.

Willis McClellan's parents named him after two young men in the community whom they admired very much. They were Willis Cole, a first cousin of his father, and McClellan Vick, an outstanding young man in the community.

Although Jim Willie Greer did not possess a great deal of money or wealth, he was a well-known and much loved man in the county. He had a reputation for being honest and upright in his work at the sawmill, cotton gin, and gristmill where he worked. He and his wife, Elizabeth

McEwen Greer were both born in Tennessee of Scotch-Irish parents.

These were honest, hard working people but times were hard and although they did all they could for their children, there were usually only the bare necessities available. As a result, all the brothers and sisters learned early in life some valuable lessons of sacrifice and hard work.

The children were expected to work picking cotton which Brother Greer loved to do lying flat on his back on the cotton sack, reaching up to pull the boles. When his sister Maude would scold him, he would soothe her ruffled spirit by telling her stories and getting her mind off his lack of work.

In the country there were always chores to be done. Young Willis was expected to go out into the woods, find the cows, round them up and drive them home late every afternoon. However, it was not all work and no play; there was always something exciting to do. The play was simple but satisfying – a game of marbles, spin-the-top, baseball, walking a rail fence barefooted in summer and an inexhaustible number of ways to play in the ice and snow in the winter time.

The first school attended by Willis McClellan was the Post Oak School in Benton County, which consisted of only one room, heated by a wood stove and with no electricity. Although it was not very comfortable for the physical body, Willis learned well the fundamentals of education, which provided a good foundation for learning in later life.

His teacher felt that six-year-old Willis was exceptional because of his extraordinary memory and perception. This special perception demonstrated itself quite well on a particular spring day. It was Saturday, and the ground was soft and damp as the warm spring sunshine was enticing it out from under the long, hard freeze of winter. As the children were playing around the yard, his youngest brother, Truman, became quite ill. Their worried mother immediately made the small child come in from play. She put him to bed and began giving him a homemade remedy. Young Willis went to his busy mother and asked her, "Mom, please give Earnestine some medicine too. I feel that she is very sick." His mother soon forgot the request because the little girl did not really appear to be sick.

As Willis McClellan went about his work and play the remainder of the day, it was with a heaviness of spirit. He would return to the house again and again to request his mother to treat Earnestine with the simple home treatment. The young mother with more work than she could get done and with one child already sick in bed, did not pay much attention to the concerned boy. It was only late the following day that the little girl began showing signs of listlessness and sickness. By 9:00 p.m. that same night, she died of an unknown malady.

Social life in the community always revolved around the home. When Willis was twelve years of age, a group of young people gathered in his home for talk and music. He made a speech about the war, then just over in 1918, that caused them all to sit still and listen. Even then he remembered events like a history book, just like his grandmother who was well known for her splendid memory.

Church life in the county consisted of once-a-month services, which were conducted by a circuit-riding Methodist preacher who pastored from three to five churches at a time. The building was just a simple one-room building with swinging oil chandeliers in the middle of the room and oil lamps with reflectors that were nailed to the unpainted wall. It was heated in the winter by a woodburning stove and cooled in the summer by palm leaf fans, if one was fortunate enough to own one. "Big Meeting Time" was one week in the summer. It would begin on a Sunday and usually closed the following Friday night. Services were both day and night, as crops were laid by and the farmers were not too busy at that time.

The church building was two miles away from the little log cabin where the Greers lived. Usually they rode in the horse-pulled wagon, but many times they would just walk. They did not attend much in the winter due to the bad weather which made the dirt roads a quagmire of deep ruts and muddy paste.

These were days of real spiritual services where many repented and were baptized. There were times of great rejoicing and worship in the services. It was during these times that there was planted in the heart of little blond-haired Willis McClellan a respect and deep longing for a Christ, whom he did not personally know.

In the early months of 1920, Brother Greer's father's health began declining rapidly, even though he was only fifty years old. Due to the hard work of the farm, it became necessary for Jim Willie Greer to begin looking for another way to earn a living for his growing family. In May 1920, Jim Greer and his oldest son, Allie, moved to Bemis, Tennessee, to work in the cotton mill. As soon as they could get a house, the rest of the family moved in June 1920. Shortly afterwards, young Willis McClellan himself went to work in the cotton mill at the age of fourteen. The industrious young man was soon promoted to be a foreman, and he served in this capacity for many years, working until the year 1942.

Jim Greer's health did not hold up long in the cotton mill, and in November of 1920 it became necessary for him to quit work altogether. Tragedy struck the struggling family a few short months later on January 10, 1921, when

Mr. Greer died. His death placed much responsibility upon the older children, especially Willis Greer. In those days there were no welfare programs or special agencies to assist families in need, so all members of the family did their part. Brother Greer's mother opened a "boarding house" and "Mammy" Greer, as she soon became known, gained a reputation in the small town of being a good cook and determined provider and protector of her little family.

The General Superintendent of the Bemis Cotton Mill soon took an interest in Brother Greer, recognizing his administrative and leadership abilities, and at age twenty he was made manager of the Supply Room, where he continued for some time.

Willis McClellan Greer soon became quite the man about town. Successful in his work and earning a good salary for those days, he bought his first car, a little brown sports model Ford Roadster. His ability to tell an interesting story, his quick wit and his keen sense of humor always seemed to make him the life of the party at social events.

It was in the year of 1925 that Willis, now nineteen, began to take a certain beautiful dark-haired girl home after the parties. Her beauty, her out-going personality and fun-loving ways, soon captivated him. It was on one of those first walks to her front door that Odis Vaughn remarked that "she was going to be an old maid." Willis Greer laughingly replied, "Perhaps I could cause you to change your mind." This he set about to do with the greatest of pleasure.

Over the next three years the young couple continued going to places of the world and doing things that unsaved youth did in the "roaring twenties." Since they both owned T Model Fords, Odis a touring car and Willis a sports model roadster, they had a lot of fun and good times together.

After dating for a year and a half, they became engaged but no specific wedding date was set.

In 1924, Brother Greer's oldest sister, Maude Greer Luther, began attending services at the Pentecostal Church in Bemis. There she made her way to an altar of repentance, received the Holy Ghost and later was baptized by Brother A. D. Gurley. None of her brothers or sisters would have anything to do with the "Holy Roller" church; but, after two years of prayer and being faithful to her Lord, her mother, Elizabeth Greer, was baptized in the precious name of Jesus. She received the Holy Ghost in 1926 while taking communion in the Bemis church. Mrs. Greer had been a member of the Methodist church for forty years at the time she received the Holy Ghost.

Events were also destined soon to make a change in the life of Willis McClellan. His mother asked him to stay home on a particular Sunday for dinner as she had asked Brother A. D. Gurley to dine. She wanted her son to meet this dynamic man of God. He consented to stay for dinner with the preacher, but it was two years later before the results of that visit came to the forefront.

Brother Gurley talked to the young man for the remainder of the afternoon, encouraging him to give his heart to the Lord and dedicate his life to serve God. For the next two years, Brother Gurley regularly requested prayer for the worldly-minded young man. He would say, "Sister Greer's boy needs to be saved. He would be useful in the kingdom of God."

Brother Greer thought about his conversation with Brother Gurley a lot, but he continued to run from the Lord until, on one March night, he became very sick.

It was on a Sunday night in March of 1928. While visiting in the home of his soon-to-be wife, Miss Odis Vaughn, he became very ill. He managed to drive himself home where he fell into bed. He was not able to get out of bed the following morning and go to his job. His mother finally prevailed upon him to let her call the preachers. Brother Gurley and Brother James W. Wallace arrived at the home around 9:00 a.m. After talking briefly with Willis, they asked if they might pray for him.

At this time, Brother Greer's mother was still running a boarding house. When the boarders came in for lunch on this day, there was none. Instead, the prayer meeting was still going on – lasting until 1:00 p.m. when Brother Greer surrendered his heart to the Lord midst great rejoicing. He was later baptized in a lake in Jackson, Tennessee where Truex Chevrolet car dealership now stands.

After several months of seeking the Holy Ghost, Brother Greer accompanied Brother Gurley to Corinth, Mississippi where he was conducting a revival. Although it was a great revival with many praying through, Brother Greer came back to Bemis empty and discouraged. He had just about decided to give up and cease seeking for the Holy Ghost. On the job the next day, Brother Greer was sitting at his desk when a man came by and enthusiastically stated, "I had a prayer meeting at my home last night and several got the Holy Ghost."

Brother Greer did not say much at the time, but later he went up into the factory where the people who had received the Holy Ghost were working, and talked with them about their experience. He later talked with the same man and asked him if he was going to have a prayer meeting that night. His reply was, "We can." The man somehow got together a group and organized a prayer meeting for that night.

Brother Greer and Odis Vaughn attended that prayer meeting on the night of August 31, 1928 in the home of D. L. Branch. There God gloriously filled Brother Greer with the Holy Ghost. Some wondered if the girl he had his heart set on would quit him now, but quite the opposite was true. Although she and her family were members of the Baptist church, when Brother Greer repented, she never cut her hair again and never went to another movie or worldly place from that day on. She jokingly said she did not marry a preacher. Two years after their marriage, she followed in his footsteps and was baptized by Brother A. D. Gurley in 1930. Shortly thereafter, she received the Holy Ghost in a camp meeting where Brother Frank Ewart was preaching.

On Saturday, September 22, 1928, Willis McClellan Greer and Odis Vaughn, along with another couple, were married in Jackson, Tennessee. Reverend Alvin West performed the ceremony as the couple sat in the back seat of an automobile. This rather humble and intimate wedding was the beginning of a loving relationship that spanned over half a century of committed devotion that was anything but uneventful.

After a short honeymoon in a Memphis hotel, the young couple returned to Bemis to live in an apartment in his mother's boarding house on the corner of Tennessee and "B" Streets.

God blessed the marriage of Willis McClellan and his lovely wife, Odis, in many, many ways. Brother Greer was soon pressed into active service in the church. He began teaching a Sunday School class even when, according to his own statement, "I didn't know Genesis from Revelation." Some four months after receiving the Holy Ghost he was appointed to serve on a committee to preside over the treasury and also to select a place and make plans for a new church building. This committee selected and secured the lots where the Bemis Pentecostal Church now stands.

He held many and varied positions in those early days under the ministry of Brother Gurley. Soon after acknowledging his call to the ministry in 1930, he began preaching in the local church, especially on Sunday nights. In 1931 he was elected the first President of the Gleaners and did a lot of preaching in the youth services where they had scores of young adults coming to the Lord. There were from fifty to sixty single young people in the youth group during this time. Under Brother Greer's direction, the youth would have cottage prayer meetings where many of them were slain under the power of God and filled with His Spirit. They just set chairs out for the altar. After prayer meeting, you would not ask, "Did anyone receive the Holy Ghost?" but you would ask, "How many received the Holy Ghost tonight?"

In 1932 Brother Greer was elected the choir director. The following year he was appointed to the church board, on which he served until he was elected pastor at the Finley Pentecostal Church in Finley, Tennessee, in late 1937. He served this church for eighteen months. Those were very trying but rewarding times. He was still working in the factory and driving the distance of 110 miles several times a week and taking his young family with him part of the time. The family now consisted of himself, his wife and three small daughters. They were Dorothy Sue, born November 9, 1929; Shirley Maxine, born November 11, 1934; and Patricia Ruth, born January 10, 1936. A son, William Wray, was born several years later on December 26, 1943.

Before and during the pastorate in the Finley church, Brother Greer also preached around the area in brush arbors, tents, street meetings, and in schoolhouses. He also preached in the local church and filled other pulpits in established churches during the absence of their pastors and for revival meetings.

In the year 1932, he attended his first General Conference of the Pentecostal Church Incorporated.

Brother Greer along with five other adults traveled, along with their luggage in a 1929 A Model Ford to Little Rock, Arkansas. The conference was held at the fairgrounds and the men's dorm was an old display barn. On the first night of the conference, Brother Greer slept on an old army cot without a sheet, quilt, pillow or mattress. On the second night, he was given a pad for the cot which made it a little more comfortable.

The great surprise and miracle at this Conference for Brother Greer happened one day when the pastor at the Little Rock Church, Brother G. H. Brown, rushed down to the conference hall and wanted someone to preach a radio broadcast. He chose Brother Greer as speaker, Sister Catherine (Mrs. M. H.) Hansford as piano player and four others to sing. How these seven people got into a 1931 A Model Ford still is a mystery. Brother Greer had never been in a studio or before a microphone. His text for this never-to-be-forgotten sermon was John 3:16. He still laughs and reminisces about the one time he was the radio preacher at a General Conference.

Even with keeping up this rather arduous schedule, he continued to hold his position in industry. He earned a promotion in 1938 to head foreman over the spinning department in the factory. His personal desire was to become the General Superintendent of the mill when the position became vacant. This would have been a very prestigious and powerful position in the small community. However, the call of God became stronger than personal desire, and he answered the call to become the assistant pastor to Brother J. W. Wallace in his home church in Bemis. While there in 1940, he was ordained to the preaching ministry by Brother A. D. Gurley and Brother J. W. Wallace.

Brother Greer relates how he and Brother Wallace would both be teaching a Bible class on Sunday morning in the same auditorium – one on each side of the middle aisle. There was not a curtain or divider of any kind down the aisle, and he would sometimes hear himself repeating a sentence a few words behind Brother Wallace. One would just have to get louder than the other to be heard.

Brother Greer served as assistant pastor to Brother Wallace, until early in 1941 when Brother Wallace resigned and moved to Nashville, Tennessee. God had a plan for Brother Wallace in Nashville, and he became founding pastor of the West Nashville Church and did pioneer preaching for all the works east of the Tennessee River since there were none at that point in time. Brother Wallace had been a steadfast, reliable leader, a man of peace and faith. The qualities of this great man very deeply and lastingly influenced Brother Greer and are still his own strong characteristics to this day.

On February 16, 1941, the Bemis Pentecostal Church elected Brother Greer to become their pastor by a 100% vote. He faithfully and diligently served in this capacity until September 2, 1962, when he resigned after twenty-one years of successful pastoring.

Immediately after his election, the church plunged into a building program and began to grow in every respect. The Sunday School grew from 130 to over 300. Revivals were held where many came to the Lord.

In the same year, 1941, on September 20, a radio broadcast live from the church was started. It was called "The Bemis Pentecostal Hour." It was said by many in the community to be the best religious broadcast at that time. It was broadcast live from the church on Sunday afternoon. All of the singing and preaching were done in front of the large audience that would gather each Sunday afternoon for the broadcast. Brother Greer went to three live broadcasts a week for a while, then to an 8:00 a.m. broadcast on Sunday morning when the entire adult choir would often come to sing and then return at 9:45 for Sunday School. Later the Sunday morning worship service was broadcast, and then the Sunday night worship service. At the conclusion of many of these Sunday night broadcasts, sinners under conviction from hearing the broadcast on their radios would make their way to the church before the altar service was over and pray through.

In the building program of 1941, the church building was completely remodeled, office space built, and a new Sunday School annex was added. Another annex was added in 1949; then the fellowship hall was built in 1955. A prayer room was added in 1958 and a new entrance to the sanctuary was completed the same year. Property surrounding the church building was acquired and made into parking lots. A parsonage was built in 1947 and the last parsonage was acquired in 1958.

Brother Greer was a progressive Sunday School oriented pastor with many ideas that were both innovative and progressive. The Sunday School more than doubled during his pastorate. At the time of his resignation in 1962, the Sunday School had ten departments with a staff of eighty-six workers. Brother Greer instituted the Pastor's Council, which met weekly. Staff meetings were held monthly, and he also had a Board of Education Meeting monthly.

During his years at Bemis, the church enjoyed the ministry of many great preachers including Brother Frank Ewart, B. H. Hite, A. D. Gurley, V. A. Guidroz, C. M. Becton, Harry Branding, N. A. Urshan, Howard A. Goss, A. T. Morgan, S. W. Chambers, G. L. Glass, Sr., Paul Gregory and many others. Many revivals lasting three to six weeks, six nights a week, were conducted by Brother and Sister Norman Paslay (when the record Sunday School attendance of 646 was set), Sister Lyndal Kraus and the Kinzie Evangelistic Party.

Brother Greer was not only busy building a church during those years, but his interest also reached out around the state and nation. He served on the District Board of the South Eastern District from March 1941, until the merger in St. Louis, Missouri, in 1945. Then he served on the newly formed board of the new Southern District of the United Pentecostal Church.

Brother Greer gives the following account of the merger conference in 1945: "The conference where the merger took place met in St. Louis, Missouri, in September 1945, in the Keil Auditorium. The vote to merge was taken by the Pentecostal Church, Incorporated in the Kiel Auditorium and the Pentecostal Assemblies of Jesus Christ met and took their vote in Brother Guinn's church. After all votes were taken the other group met with the Pentecostal Church Incorporated in the Kiel Auditorium, I remember that suddenly the conference was filled with people who were strangers – people I had not seen before. But of course, through the years I have become acquainted with them and learned to love, work with, and appreciate many of them greatly."

The new Southern District consisted of Tennessee, Mississippi, and Alabama. One of the first things they did was to purchase a Bible school in Tupelo, Mississippi, which became known as the Tupelo Bible Institute.

At the district conference in Bemis, Tennessee, in April 1949, the conference delegates voted to make each state a separate district. Brother Greer was elected by 100% vote as the first district superintendent of the Tennessee District, which office he held for thirty years. He was elected to the superintendent's office fifteen times – this by acclamation as long as it was allowed. He had opposition only two times in the entire thirty years.

His first official act was to call a board meeting. They voted to send out a letter to all the preachers, but they discovered they did not own a postage stamp. This has been laughed about many times.

Throughout his ministry, Brother Greer attended over forty General Conferences, not missing one of the entire time he was on the General Board. He recalls many times when both General and District Board meetings have lasted throughout the night as they wrestled with problems and difficult situations.

When Tennessee became a separate district in 1949, the old Southern District had a camp ground in Mississippi, and that usual procedure of attending this camp was followed for the summer of 1949. After that year, the Tennessee District sold their interest in the camp ground, which made further meetings there impossible. However, the people of Tennessee had an inherent love for camp meetings. It was this particular region, over half a century before that witnessed the great religious fervor in the camp meetings of that day. Tennessee had been apart of the old camp meeting league that was formed under the able leadership of Brother A. D. Gurley in the year of 1941, which later became the official camp meeting of the Southern District of the United Pentecostal Church.

Naturally, with such a background, it was imperative that a place for camp meetings be found. In April of 1951, land was purchased and an able building superintendent, Brother J. W. Wallace, went to work. By July of the same year, he had a rustic tabernacle, dining hall and other buildings for the first great camp meeting of the Tennessee District. "Holiness Hill," as it has been named by the local residents, is situated on a heavily wooded hill overlooking the beautiful Tennessee River, Brother Norman and Sister Mary Alice Pasley were the evangelists for that first and memorable camp meeting.

Property was purchased in Jackson, Tennessee, in 1972 for a District Office building. The building has been completed and the Tennessee District can well be proud of this modern brick structure.

Brother Greer pastored the Bemis church and was Tennessee District Superintendent for over thirteen years before he became full time as superintendent. There came the time when the load was too heavy and one responsibility had to go. Brother Greer thought that after over twenty-one years as pastor, the greater challenge was in the district, so this was the choice in September 1962.

As superintendent he has traveled innumerable miles, preached countless sermons. Officiated in scores of special services such as note burning of church property, anniversaries of churches all over the district. No church was ever too small or too large for him to visit.

In April 1974, the district officials and ministers celebrated the 25th Anniversary of the Tennessee District and also Brother Greer's 25th Anniversary as superintendent. There were special banquets, meetings, gifts and a lovely silver-covered commemorative album, which portrayed in pictures and words the involvement of the Tennessee District, United Pentecostal Church in the worldwide work of the kingdom of God.

Sister Greer's health began to fail and Brother Greer could never feel free to leave her when she had been so true when he had needed her so much through the years. Under the cares of life and long years of service, he resigned the district superintendency in the midst of his thirtieth year of office.

Brother Greer spent the next five and one-half years caring for his beloved companion. He would preach close by and go on long trips when she was able to go along. His dear wife for over fifty years was promoted to glory on August 25, 1983.

Brother Greer is now Superintendent Emeritus of the Tennessee District and an honorary member of the General Board. He still travels widely in the district filling pulpits for special services and days. He is greatly enjoying serving with his "son in the gospel" and great-nephew, Brother Bill Luther (grandson to Brother Greer's sister, Maude, who was the first member of his family to receive the Holy Ghost) in the Bemis Pentecostal Church. He is teacher of the Men's Bible Class, where exciting things are happening. He taught a Bible Class in the same place over fifty years ago, and laughingly relates that "history is repeating itself."

He is very active in the hospital and sick visitation and has been actively involved in door to door contacts in a very successful "Enroll to Grow" campaign. He has a study at the church with his "old desk" and study books installed.

Brother Greer is a man of principle and strong convictions – firm and uncompromising with that which he knows to be wrong – yet kind, considerate and gentle with those who need help. He is a man of phenomenal wisdom, a lover of peace, and gifted with an ability to deal with complex problems and help resolve differences between people. His distinctive sense of humor and benevolent smile have made him a man much loved, appreciated, and highly respected by those who know him.

EPILOGUE:

On September 10, 1984, Brother Greer married Merle Dawson, a faithful and dedicated lady from the Lighthouse

Pentecostal Church. They shared a number of productive years of ministry until their health began to wane. Despite his failing health, at ninety-two years of age, Brother Greer was able to attend the Easter Service on April 4, 1999 at the Bemis Pentecostal Church. In this service, Reverend Nathaniel Urshan, General Superintendent of the United Pentecostal Church, paid tribute to Brother Greer as he brought God's Word to the church. Pastor Carl McKellar, the church board, and the membership honored Brother Greer by bestowing on him the title of "Bishop W. M. Greer."

On Wednesday night, April 7, 1999, as the Tennessee District celebrated its 50th Anniversary at the Bemis Church where the District was formed in 1949, Brother Greer was able to be present and accept recognition as the first Superintendent of the Tennessee District. In this service following a skit depicting some of his special work and words from Reverend Nathaniel Urshan and Reverend Paul Price of California, Brother Greer preached an anointed message to an overflow congregation. This was to be Brother Greer's last sermon. His body became weaker. He entered the hospital in Jackson, Tennessee on November 1, 1999. Two days later on November 3rd, with part of his family and two close friends at his bedside, he quietly closed his eyes and his tired heart stopped. He left his earthly habitation to enter into that rest which he had prepared for many years ago.

58   Tennessee District Heritage

The W. M. Greer Family, 1944.

Rev. and Mrs. W. M. Greer, Fiftieth Wedding Anniversary

ELMER E. McNATT
By Mary Jackson

Elmer E. McNatt was born October 21, 1908 in Bemis, Tennessee. He was the oldest son of Alvin and Orena Marsh McNatt. His family included six sisters and one brother -- Ethel, Virgie, Ersell, Birdie Mai, Clara, Alvin, Jr., and Marie. Elmer grew up and was educated in Bemis.

On December 15, 1928, he married Elizabeth Alline Burton. Rev. A. D. Gurley, pastor of Bemis Pentecostal Church, performed the wedding ceremony in Madison County. To this union God added two girls, Bessie and Helen. Elmer was employed as a taxi driver. This was an interesting job, which he enjoyed very much. He also worked for a candy company as a salesman. His business ability was evident early in his life.

Elmer and Alline began attending a tent revival in Bemis where Rev. A. D. Gurley was the speaker. The anointed singing and ministry of the Word reached his heart. He was outside the tent when conviction melted his heart, and he went to the altar and repented. He was baptized in Jesus Name and later received the Holy Ghost. He was very zealous in his new found experience and his sweet relationship with Jesus. He began his ministry in 1937. His first sermon was preached at Wilson

Schoolhouse, and his first pastorate was in Dyersburg, Tennessee. After Rev. W. M. Greer resigned the Finley Church, he was elected pastor there and served for about two years.

In June 1940, new hope, new courage, and great faith came to a group of Pentecostal people who were unorganized and without a pastor. A cry for help brought Rev. A. D. Gurley, then Superintendent of the Southeastern District of the Pentecostal Church, Inc., and Rev. E. E. McNatt, Pastor at Finley and Dyersburg, to the rescue of the troubled group of Oneness Pentecostal saints. In May, Brother Gurley and Brother McNatt held a four-week revival for this group. When the revival was over, they held a business meeting and asked Brother McNatt to become their pastor, which he did in June. This church was located at Fourth and Keel Streets in Memphis. Seventy-four members made up the newly organized church and they affiliated with the Pentecostal Church, Inc.

Under Brother McNatt's leadership the church enjoyed a gradual growth in number and spirituality. During his pastorate there, approximately nine hundred were baptized with the Holy Ghost. A number of ministers were licensed from this group, some of whom were Rev. J. E. Ross, Rev. C. L. Crum, Rev. Charles Shanks, Rev. O. W. Williams, Rev. Rexie Wilcox, Rev. M. D. Deal, Rev. Vernon Greer, Rev. A. M. Launis, Sister Ruth Cook, Sister Kathryn Baroni, Sister Pearl Groves and Rev. J. H. Cain.

When the merger of the Pentecostal Church, Inc. and Pentecostal Assemblies of Jesus Christ took place and the organization became the United Pentecostal Church, Brother McNatt was appointed the first official head of the Sunday School Department. This was in the year 1948. Then in 1949 at the General Conference, he was elected to the position. He held this office until he resigned in 1954.

In 1955 he was again elected Sunday School Director and served until his resignation shortly before the General Conference in 1958.

When the Southern District of the United Pentecostal Church was divided into three separate districts in 1949 and Tennessee became a district, Brother McNatt was elected the first District Secretary. However his burden was for Sunday School, so after a couple of years, he and Brother J. O. Wallace exchanged offices. Brother Wallace was elected District Secretary and Brother McNatt became District Sunday School Director. He held this office from 1951 until his resignation in 1958. Along with his District responsibilities, he was also serving as the International Sunday School Director. As the International Director he planned Sunday School Conventions in different areas of the United States. He was extremely active in promoting teacher training programs and also wrote a book on Sunday School organization entitled, "The Pentecostal Sunday School."

While filling these positions in the General organization and the District, he was pastoring the First Pentecostal Church in Memphis. He had high hopes of building the largest church in Tennessee and had a great measure of success. He resigned the Memphis church in 1962. Besides his pastoring and the Sunday School work, his ministry included much work at the Tennessee District Camp Ground at Perryville, Tennessee.

Brother McNatt was a very successful evangelist and ministered in many churches winning souls for the Lord. He was a man of great faith and a great preacher of faith. Many miracles of healing happened during his ministry. One young boy, Sonny Prater, had what was called lock-jaw at that time. He was given little chance of survival and Brother McNatt prayed for him and God healed him. Sonny still lives in Memphis and testifies to this healing. Another instance was when they had said Sister Ruth Cook was dead, and when prayer was made she came back to life. On another occasion, Brother Hawkins of the Memphis church took Brother McNatt and some other men to Mississippi to pray for his dad. He had had a stroke and was paralyzed. They had prayer for him and went into another room to pray for Brother Hawkins' mother, and while praying for her, the dad got out of bed, dressed and walked into her room completely healed. One lady had a crooked arm and when Brother McNatt baptized her she was healed. These are only a few of the wonderful miracles of his ministry.

After resigning from the First Pentecostal Church in Memphis, Brother McNatt assisted in building another Pentecostal Church in the Frayser area of Memphis. His health was failing and his last few years were spent with his family. He passed away on June 13, 1969. Rev. C. M. Becton and Rev. J. O. Wallace preached his funeral in Memphis.

A Great Baptismal Service

Tennessee District Heritage 63

The McNatt Family: E.E. McNatt, wife, Ailene; daughters, Bessie and Helen.

Bro. McNatt's well-known radio ministry was on station WMPS of Memphis.

Rev. and Mrs. E. E. McNatt at an anniversary service in Memphis.

J. O. WALLACE
Autobiography

James Onell Wallace was born on October 8, 1915, in Decatur County, Tennessee close to Luray. He was the second son of James Wells Wallace and Allie Izana Robbins Wallace. The family lived in a small country cottage with no amenities on the land that J. W. sharecropped. Water came from the cistern by the back porch. Coal oil lamps provided the light except on one memorable occasion when J. W. was washing his tired feet on the back porch. A light from an unexplained source suddenly shone on his bare feet, reminding him of the scripture, "How beautiful upon the mountain are the feet of him that bringeth good tidings of God, and publisheth salvation ..." Isaiah 52:7. At this time J. W. was an exhorter in the community church.

In 1918, a little known oneness Pentecostal minister, Brother Kennedy, came to their community and held a "brush arbor" revival. Both Brother and Sister Wallace received the Holy Ghost. They were subsequently asked to leave the community Methodist church.

Later the family moved to Bemis where Rev. A. D. Gurley pastored the Pentecostal Church. The Wallaces became active in the church, and J. W. served as assistant pastor for 15 years. When J. O., "Onell", was 16, he received the Holy Ghost in a summer tent revival meeting and was baptized in Jesus' name in the Bemis swimming pool.

J. O. went to work part-time in the Bemis Cotton Mill at 14, then full-time at 16 on the second shift, 2:00 – 10:00 p.m. After graduation from high school, he attended Lambuth College. Some time later he decided to transfer to Draughn's College in Memphis with a major in accounting. He attended church at 4th and Keel where Brother E. E. McNatt was pastoring. There J. O. served as Secretary and Treasurer as well as Youth Leader.

He completed the accounting course and received a certificate from Draughn's College in the spring of 1940 and went to work for an elderly Certified Public Accountant uptown in Memphis. About this time the war in Europe was looking very serious, with Hitler's threats including the United States. So young men were required to register for the military. A low draft number made J. O. likely to be called in three months. It was November by then. He decided to leave his new job and go home for a few weeks before Uncle Sam called.

"In those days we were not accustomed to using the telephone for communication. When I arrived in Jackson and walked to the bus stop for the Bemis bus, I met my father coming from the opposite direction. He asked, 'Where are you going?' I replied, 'Where are you going?'" After the answers were exchanged, they both decided to take off for Nashville the following week.

The Nashville Crusade was set in motion. Jobs were secured, and cottage prayer meetings and Bible studies began. After only a few weeks, lots were purchased on the corner of 51st and Delaware Avenues. The first public service began in a tent on these lots the first of April 1941. J. W. served as Pastor with J. O. as his assistant and the first

Sunday School Superintendent. There were 42 in Sunday School the first Sunday. To pay their bills, J. W. had gotten a machinist job at Werthan Bag Company, while J. O. got a job with Spur Oil Company as bookkeeper. A revival brought in two good families.

On May 21, 1941, there was a letter from the President of the United States stating that Uncle Sam was needing some recruits. "This meant a trip to Memphis to join my group from the draft board." They were shipped immediately by troop train to San Diego, California. Meanwhile, J. O. had been writing daily to a young girl, Mary Martha Hardwick, in Finley. In July 1942 they were married in Santa Barbara, California by the will of God.

In God's providence, J. O. was assigned back to Nashville about a mile from his father's home and the West Nashville Pentecostal church. Their first child, James Onell Wallace, Jr. was born in September 1944. That same summer while still in uniform, J. O. and his father pitched a tent in a pasture in Goodlettsville. This began the second United Pentecostal Church east of the Tennessee River. J. O. was still a soldier but was discharged after the war in October 1945. Utilizing the help of Uncle Sam and the G. I. Bill of Rights, J. O. entered Bob Jones College, which was located in Cleveland, Tennessee at that time.

A daughter, Margaret Jane "Margie" was born in 1947. In 1948, J. O. began teaching in the Pentecostal Bible Institute in Tupelo, Mississippi. A year later the Wallaces moved back to Nashville and began a church on Rose and Sadler in the Woodbine community of south Nashville. Nine persons attended the first Sunday. He asked his young brother-in-law, L. H. Hardwick, Jr., to help with the church.

The year 1949 was special to the people of Tennessee. The old Southern District of the United Pentecostal Church was divided and Tennessee became a district. At this conference in Bemis, J. O. was elected as the first Sunday School Director of the new Tennessee District. He held this office for two years.

In 1951, J. O. was chosen to be the District Secretary of the Tennessee District under the leadership of Rev. W. M. Greer, District Superintendent. "What about Woodbine?" he asked his father. "Leave it with Brother Hardwick," was the answer.

In January 1951 the Wallaces moved to Bemis to set up a district office and also to serve as Brother Greer's assistant pastor in the Bemis Pentecostal Church. Their third child, John Hardwick, "Jack", Wallace was born on July 3rd while J. O. and other Pentecostals were at the Tennessee Campground for the first service in the new camp.

In September the Wallaces moved the district office to the campground, and J. O. also served as campground superintendent. In addition, J. O. enrolled in George Peabody College for Teachers and commuted to Nashville to finish his Bachelor of Arts degree. In November Rev. A. T. Morgan, General Superintendent of the United Pentecostal Church, asked J. O. to come to the U. P. C. headquarters in St. Louis, Missouri to manage the Pentecostal Publishing House. So J. O. resigned his position in Tennessee, dropped out of Peabody, and moved the family to St. Louis in November. Their fourth child, Jeffrey Wells, was born in 1952.

In the meantime, J. W. Wallace had used the last of his strength in building the new brick church on 51st and Delaware in Nashville as well as supervising the building of the campground facilities. In October 1953 at the General Conference of the U.P.C. in St. Louis, J. W. talked with his son, "I need help, Onell. Will you come back to Nashville and assist me with the West Nashville Church?" After having been reappointed as P.P.H. manager, J. O. resigned, and the family moved to Nashville.

In 1956 J. O. resigned the West Nashville church, and the family moved to assume the pastorate of the Oak Ridge U. P. C. While pastoring Oak Ridge, J. O. invited Evangelist Ernie Jolley to hold a revival, and Sunday School attendance more than tripled. Also in Oak Ridge, the Wallace's fifth child, Rosemary, was born.

In 1958 at the U. P. C. General Conference, J. O. was appointed General Sunday School Director. At that time the family moved back to Nashville where Mary served as director of the West Nashville Kindergarten which they had established in 1951. J. O. traveled for the Sunday School Department and commuted to the office in St. Louis. Their last child, Joseph Glenn, was born in 1962.

The Wallaces moved to Collinsville, Illinois, after the U.P.C. bought property on Interstate 70 to build a new headquarters. After Brother Morgan's death, the organization sold the Collinsville property and bought land in Hazelwood, Missouri, where they built a beautiful new facility. J. O. served as General Sunday School Director for 17 years. During this time a great deal of interest in Sunday School changes were accomplished. A number of effective attendance and new methods of class arrangements helped greatly in the classroom. The use of weekend workshops and demonstrations aided in upgrading hundreds of Sunday Schools in a short time. It was indeed an exciting time for our teachers. At this time the U.P.C. Sunday school curriculum, Word Aflame Publications was launched.

The world wide thrust attendance drive began to receive increasing interest in many foreign countries, so much that J. O. and Mary made two "Round the World Tours" in 1974 and 1975 visiting 16 countries teaching the new Sunday School methods.

After resigning in 1975, the Wallaces began teaching at Jackson College of Ministries, formerly the Pentecostal Institute, with Rev. T. L. Craft as President in Jackson, Mississippi.

A year later the Wallaces moved back to Nashville and pastored a small church. In the meantime Mary, who had served as editor of kindergarten curriculum of U.P.C. Sunday School materials, was asked to return to Hazelwood as full-time editor of nursery-kindergarten curriculum.

About a year later Brother N. A. Urshan, General Superintendent of the U.P.C., asked J. O. to again manage the Pentecostal Publishing House. He served in this position for the next 12 years. During that time P. P. H. was greatly expanded.

In 1994 the Wallaces moved back to Tennesee where J. O. at 83 is enjoying good health and retirement. Their six children, their spouses and twelve grandchildren enjoy holidays and vacations with the Wallaces. J. O. declares that life comes down to two words, "God" and "family."

J. O. Wallace, manager of the Pentecostal Publishing House in Hazelwood, Missouri, in his World Evangelism Center Office.

70 Tennessee District Heritage

The Wallace's and the Fred Kinzie's on an international Sunday School Seminar in Pakistan and Indai in 1976.

Rev & Mrs. J.O. Wallace with Jeff and Jack.

The entire Wallace Family gathered to help J.O. Wallace celebrate his 80th birthday in 1995!

JOSEPH O. MOORE
Autobiography: November 1998

In the early months of 1920 my father, A. O. Moore and my mother, Lydia Sonnenberg, met and got acquainted at a railway station while waiting for their trains to take them to their respective destinations. Lydia was traveling with a lady missionary, Sister Mae Ira. They were married on July 15 of that year. My sister, Naomi, and I are the children of that couple.

I was born in Hot Springs, Arkansas on July 27, 1923. My mother died when I was only eight days old. After her death, my father arranged for our care in Christian homes while he traveled in itinerant evangelistic ministry. In 1925, he was able to place both of us in the home of the V. H. Cross family up in Ontario, Canada, so we could be together. In 1926 Dad sailed from Montreal, Canada to spend two years in India, working with missionaries there. Upon his return to the U. S. A. he met Josephine Gilstrap in Oakland, California. They were married in June of 1929 and immediately began the journey to Ontario to be joined with Naomi and me. They arrived in October, and we became a family again. In the ensuing years, five more children were added to the family, two boys and three girls. We spent a few months back in the U. S. A. and in May of

1930 moved to Picton, Ontario, in response to the call my father received to pastor the church there. I attended public school and one year of high school in Picton.

I returned to live with the Cross family in 1937 and stayed there until the end of 1940. My family had moved from Picton to El Paso, Texas in 1938. In 1941 I went home to El Paso and enrolled in school there to complete my high school education.

I had given my heart to the Lord in a children's service at the district camp meeting. I was baptized and later received the Holy Ghost in the prayer room in Picton at age nine or ten. Early in life I began to feel the call of God, but I was not interested in becoming a preacher. But during the school years of 1941 and '42, in addition to school work, I was involved with our church young people in street meeting ministry and revival meetings in the church. In this spiritual environment, the call of God became definite and urgent. God, by His grace, enabled me to pray this issue through and say, "not my will but Thine be done." I acknowledged the call to the ministry and prepared to obey the Lord.

I graduated from El Paso Tech on Monday night, May 26, 1942. I boarded a Greyhound bus on Tuesday morning and began my ministry as a young evangelist in Albuquerque, New Mexico that night. My travels during the next four years took me to churches in several states and into the provinces of Manitoba and Ontario in Canada. All of my travel was by train and bus because these were the war years and I could not afford to own or operate a car. I received my first ministerial license with the Pentecostal Church, Inc., in 1942 and was ordained at the General Conference in Jonesboro, Arkansas in 1944.

During these years of travel I had developed a friendship with Doris Gurley, the eldest daughter of Rev.

and Mrs. A. D. Gurley. We were married in Corinth, Mississippi in June 1946. We left immediately to go to Ontario where I had ministry engagements for the summer. I had serious health problems during the fall and winter – a bleeding ulcer – and was unable to preach for several months. In May of 1947, we returned to Corinth, Mississippi.

As I regained my health, I became able to minister again. In the summer of 1947, I accepted the call to pastor the church in Henderson, Tennessee. Our son, Keith, was born in August and we moved to Henderson in September. Our two daughters, Troyce and Trudy, were born in 1951 and 1953, respectively.

I believe the ten and a half years in Henderson were some of the most important years in the development of my ministry. They were extremely busy, and sometimes stressful, with life experiences as well as the duties of pastoral ministry and district involvement.

Prior to 1949 I had served as Youth President of the Southern District, which included Tennessee, Mississippi and Alabama, of which Brother A. D. Gurley was the District Superintendent. After the Tennessee District was formed in 1949 I became very involved in all of the district programs, in addition to my pastoral duties. My first official position was as Youth President, then I was appointed as assistant to Brother Kenneth Reeves. He had been elected to be District Secretary-Treasurer following the resignation of Brother J. O. Wallace. At the next district conference I was elected as the District Secretary-Treasurer when Brother Reeves declined a second term. During these years I also served one term as National Youth President, 1949-51.

The years in Henderson, along with all the good memories, are also remembered for some other events. I had recurrences of my ulcer problem, which necessitated emergency surgery in 1951. In 1956, the problem had returned and again surgery was required. Six days later there were serious complications and a second surgery was performed The doctors gave little hope for my recovery, but the prayers of God's people were answered and I recovered. God has added many years to my life and now at age 75, I still enjoy very good health.

In January 1952, we had a car accident as we returned home from the opening service of our district youth convention. Some of us suffered serious injuries, the most serious were Brother Calvin Rigdon, Doris and myself. Thank the Lord we all recovered. In March of the same year a violent tornado struck Henderson causing much destruction and loss of life. Our basement church was demolished. We relocated and the brick church on Barham Street was erected and dedicated. In later years the Sunday School addition, the parsonage, and fellowship hall were added to the property, as other pastors followed us there.

During the Henderson years, as God blessed and the church grew in numbers, some of the new converts were young men who were called into the ministry. Some of these were Billy Cupples, Darnell McCollum, Jesse Plunk and Dick Kitchen. I expect to see all of them in glory some day.

The years that I served as District Secretary-Treasurer were learning and growing years of ministry for me. Brother W. M. Greer was the man under whom and with whom I served. We traveled many miles together, had wonderful hours of fellowship. Sometimes it seemed that we sweat blood and tears as we dealt with the many challenges associated with a growing district, planting new churches, developing a campground, planning conferences and camp meetings, convening district board meetings, and dealing with local church needs and problems. Brother Greer was a spiritual mentor to me and I felt like I was a Timothy working with a modern Apostle Paul. To this day I have the deepest appreciation and respect for this great man.

In February of 1958 I accepted a call to Oak Ridge and our family moved to that Atomic City. Our stay there terminated much sooner than we anticipated. In the summer of 1959, I received a call to pastor the church in Toronto, Ontario. This produced very mixed emotions for the entire family, but after prayerful consideration we felt it to be the will of God to make the move. We arrived in Toronto in September, got the children enrolled in school and settled into our ministry there.

The details of these years are not pertinent to the history of the Tennessee District, so I will give only a brief summary here. I served the Toronto church until the end of 1962. I then moved to Picton, Ontario to pastor the church there and was there until July of 1971. The next move was back to Toronto. In October of 1972, we pioneered a new work in Scarborough, a city at that time of over 300,000. It is now a part of the Megacity of Toronto. I completed my years of pastoral ministry when I retired as pastor of Life Tabernacle in July 1993 when I turned 70.

During these years in Ontario I have, in addition to pastoral ministry, served as District Superintendent of the Ontario District of the United Pentecostal Church for ten years, 1963-73. From 1984 to 1996, I served as the District Presbyter of Ontario for the Apostolic Church of Pentecost of Canada. During our stay in Picton, the Apostolic Missionary Institute operated in the local church facilities beginning in 1967. I served as President of this Bible School from 1967-71, in addition to my other duties.

Doris and I celebrated our 50th wedding anniversary in 1996. We are now living in retirement here in Toronto. I am thankful for the abundant grace of God that has enabled me to serve the Lord and His Church for the past 56 years. The statement of the Apostle Paul in 1 Corinthians 15:10 is also my testimony: "But by the grace of God I am what I am, and His grace toward me was not in vain."

Epilogue:

This autobiography was written by Brother J. O. Moore in November 1998. At that time, he wrote in a personal letter of his thanks to the Lord for the health he and his wife, Doris, had at their stage in life. In the next year, he learned that he had colon cancer. After nearly a year of treatments and surgery, he no longer desired to live and asked that all life support machines be taken off. His statement to the doctors and his family was "I have a better home than this, and I'm ready to go." God granted that wish on February 12, 2000 in the late afternoon. His funeral was held at Benfield Memorial Church in Toronto, Canada on February 14, at 1:00 p.m.

Rev. & Mrs. J. O. Moore, about 1965

J. O. Moore and Norman Pasley, Perryville Camp Ground in 1959.

JAMES HERBERT AUSTIN
By Joel Austin

James Herbert Austin was born to Arthur and Jennie Sowell Austin on March 14, 1911 in Bemis, Tennessee. He attended school in Bemis.

Brother Austin told that he remembered in 1916, a minister named B. H. Hite who brought a small tent and seats to Bemis and held a revival. Brother Hite, a man full of the Holy Ghost, had been healed of tuberculosis, which was fatal in those days. He preached old-time holiness and divine healing. The town of Bemis was stirred; they had never heard such powerful preaching. It was told that there were 150 people filled with the Holy Ghost during this meeting, among whom were Brother Austin's dad and his uncle, Vester Austin.

As a child, Brother Austin told of getting out of bed, getting down on his knees and praying to the Lord to be patient with him and let no harm come to him until he was older. Brother Austin said that there was a seed planted in his heart, and he had a difficult time going the way of the world.

As a young man, Brother Austin worked in the textile plant in Bemis. One day he was looking out the window from the plant, and he saw a beautiful young girl walking down the street. He inquired, found out who she was and drove by her house. He walked to her door and asked her for a date. She turned him down that first time, but the next time he asked, she said "yes." He and this lady (Lois Patrick) went together for one year or more, and he asked her to marry him. At that time she was a member of the Church of Christ. He knew that he loved her, and on May 10, 1930 they were married and were very happy.

An acquaintance of Brother Austin's asked him one day if he believed that the Holy Ghost was for everyone, and he read Acts 2:38 to him. This caused Brother Austin to spend more time reading his Bible. Others began witnessing to Brother Austin; then one night, he dreamed of the coming of Jesus. This had a profound effect on his life. On July 8, 1934, Brother Austin went to a revival meeting at the Bemis Pentecostal Church where Brother A. D. Gurley was the evangelist. Brother Gurley preached on the "Six Steps to the Throne." It was that night that Brother Austin ran to the altar and called on the Lord. The pastor of the church, Brother J. W. Wallace was a great influence on his life. He told Brother Austin that Jesus loved him and wanted to save him. Brother Austin believed Brother Wallace, and the joy of the Lord filled his soul. He asked to be baptized in His name, and so he was. Brother Austin's wife was stirred by all that was happening to her husband. She also went to the altar and gave her life to Jesus and was baptized. In time, both Brother and Sister Austin received the baptism of the Holy Ghost.

It wasn't long until God began to deal with Brother Austin about preaching the gospel. He and his brother-in-law, Brother Allie Greer, and a few other men were out fishing, and he couldn't catch anything because all he could do was weep as the Spirit moved upon him. The Lord spoke to him and told him that he would make him a fisherman for him. He went home and told his precious wife. They both began to cry, and Brother Austin could not even eat for days. Brother Austin went on street meetings and God blessed him when he tried to speak.

Brother and Sister Austin were blessed with three sons and two daughters. There were many times God healed him and Sister Austin and their children, shielding them from death on several occasions. Mary Elizabeth, Margaret Sue, James Titus and Joel Patrick were all born in Bemis, Tennessee. William Emmett was born in Finley, Tennessee. When the family moved to pastor the Dyersburg and Finley churches, there were not sufficient funds for Brother Austin to go full time with the churches. Brother Austin would sell Bibles, and the children would work in the fields, run paper routes, etc., to supplement the income of the family. Brother Austin wanted his wife and children to have the necessary things of life, so by the children helping, Brother Austin had more time to preach God's word. Many souls were added to these churches. A new parsonage was built in Finley and the church building was remodeled. New Sunday school rooms were built and the auditorium expanded. Brother Austin returned to Dyersburg to pastor until his retirement in the fall of 1981. God blessed his efforts in Hohenwald and returning to Dyersburg. Brother Austin was one of the first five district board members elected in 1949 when Tennessee became a separate district of the United Pentecostal Church. He served in this office until 1956. He was home Missions Director from 1956 to 1959.

Brother Austin was not just limited to pastoring. He preached in jails, penitentiaries, held revivals in schools, brush arbors, tents, churches, street meetings, and anywhere that he was given an opportunity. Brother Austin saw many people saved, some of which were of other religious beliefs. He did not want to give up on anyone.

Brother and Sister Austin's daughter, Sue, married Kenneth Hughey while they were in Finley. They lost one child in death, but were later blessed by God with a son whom they named Kenny. Kenneth was from the Finley area and served in the Air Force for 30 years. While Kenny was just a small child, his dad was called to serve as an airline pilot in the Vietnam War. His plane was shot down, and he was held as a prisoner of war for over six years. Many prayers were prayed for him, and everyone was so happy when he was able to return home. As time went on, Kenny grew up and married a young lady named Julie. They now have two daughters, and all this family now lives in Manhattan Beach, California.

Joel married Melba Lewis in Corinth, Mississippi. Melba was from Gilbertown, Alabama. Joel was in the Air Force for some 20 years. They lost two sons in early death, but God blessed them with a precious daughter, Kathie Darlene. Kathie graduated from Jackson College of Ministries. God blessed her with a great talent for singing. Joel was vice-president and administrator for six and a half years at Jackson College of Ministries. Kathie is married to John Moreland, they have a daughter and son and reside in Louisville, Kentucky where they are active in the Lord's work. Joel and Melba have begun a new work for God in Chattanooga, Tennessee, and God is blessing.

Titus married Pat Harrington of Hohenwald, Tennessee. He also spent time in the Air Force. God blessed their marriage with three precious children, Victor, Keith and Mitzie. They have lived in three different states. Titus and Pat are happy to have Mitzie and her husband in Hohenwald where she teaches school. Titus and Pat have five grandchildren.

Mary Elizabeth married Hubert Mosley on June 13, 1958 at the Hohenwald Church. Hubert was a local business man there for many years. His first wife was an aunt of Joel's wife (Melba). She died of cancer in 1957, having three grown children (one daughter who had just finished high school, one son in medical school and one son who was just finishing high school), and also a young son who was only ten years old. Elizabeth taught him the ways of the Lord. Brother Austin had so much influence on this child (Jackie). Jackie had a desire to attend one of our Bible colleges. This desire was granted and he attended and graduated from Tupelo Bible College. God called him into the ministry and years later he pastored his home church in Gilbertown, Alabama. One of the best revivals the church ever experienced was with Brother Austin as the evangelist.

William was the last of Brother Austin's children to marry. His bride was Ruth Ann Douglas, who was a school teacher. She was raised in the Pentecostal truth. William also served his time in the Air Force. God blessed them with a daughter, LeAnn, who at this time is attending college.

Not only did Brother Austin have the privilege of baptizing some of his children, but also his in-laws, Kenneth, Melba, Pat and Hubert and grandchildren. Step-grandson, Jackie, was baptized at the Dyersburg Church in 1966. All of Brother and Sister Austin's children and their families attend churches in their home areas.

Mary Elizabeth says she never remembers her parents not living for God. "Our home had love. I remember our times of family devotion, going to church, our times of eating and having fun together. Dad would want me to play the piano in church before my feet could touch the pedals. We'd all sing from time to time. Daddy enjoyed playing the French harp. One of his favorite songs was 'When I Take my Vacation in Heaven'. He'd play the harp and I'd play the piano along with him. Dad loved to sing also. There would be times when I'd go with him to preach a revival. Daddy was the greatest pastor I ever had. He was a loving dad and lived a life above reproach. He always wanted his children to be good examples before the church and entire community. His dream was to have his three sons preach. Our brother Joel is now preaching and we are all very proud of him. I just wish Daddy was alive to hear him, but he passed on December 2, 1994 of Alzheimer's Disease."

The J. H. Austin Family: J.H. Austin (seated), Titus, Sis. Austin, Joel, Sue, Elizabeth, and William.

Tennessee District Heritage 83

J. H. and Lois Austin beside their nice new car.

J. H. Austin with L. H. Hardwick at Perryville Campground.

Bro. & Sis. Austin and others
April 1941

E. J. DOUGLAS
By Jeff Douglas and Ann Luther

Elco Jefferson Douglas was born in the small community of Beacon, Decatur County, Tennessee, on January 24, 1888. He was one of seven children, three sons and four daughters, born to Jefferson and Frances Douglas.

Reared on the farm, E. J. and his brothers were required to do all sorts of farm work including plowing, feeding the stock and maintenance work. His sisters contributed their share of labor to the welfare of the home by cleaning, canning and sewing. Because of inconvenient transportation and lack of financial means, Mr. Douglas could provide his children with only a grammar school education.

Pa and Ma Douglas were very strict members of the Cumberland Presbyterian Church. They were very particular about the activities in their home. Family life did not include swearing, dancing, card playing, or any other worldly ways. As the children grew older, they also united with the same faith. E. J. was the last of the family to give his heart to God.

E. J. Douglas' conversion took place when he was fifteen. It happened one morning on "hog killing" day as he and his brothers were preparing the meat to hang in the old-fashioned smokehouse. (The process of curing meat in those days was to suspend the pork in midair, then to smoke it with smoldering hickory chips.) On his way down near their fresh water spring for some small short sticks to pierce through the ham hocks, E. J. became overwhelmed by the conviction that had been laying heavily upon his soul for days. Blinded by tears of remorse and repentance, he stumbled through the wooded area until he came to the roots of a giant white oak tree. There, under its sheltering branches, he knelt and cried out to the Lord for deliverance from the terrible burden of sin. When he felt the burden lifted, he rejoiced in the Lord.

He decided at that time to keep his experience with God a secret; however, this did not seem to be God's will. A few months later he and his parents attended a revival in the Presbyterian Church. During the altar call the preacher asked each individual if he was a Christian. As the preacher came down the line, several thoughts began to run through the mind of the shy young man. Should he leave the building? No. He knew what his father would do to him when they arrived home. The razor strap was most popular in those days. Should he reply with an evasive answer? No. He could not lie about it. He was "on the spot," so when he was asked the question by the preacher, he meekly nodded his head in the affirmative. When the services were ended, his parents questioned him further. They rejoiced when he told them of his experience in the woods.

"But I don't seem satisfied," the puzzled young man stated. "There seems to be something else I need."

The perplexed parents, not knowing any other answer to give the seeking young man, advised him to join the church and find satisfaction in working for the church. When he did, to his dismay, he found that it failed to fulfill the void in his spirit.

For a time he was devoted to his new-found religious faith. He sang in the choir and led in public prayer. At times he shouted, raising his hands in praise to God. He continued for some time to attend church and take part in worship and activities. However, the void that he had felt in his heart grew stronger as his faith grew weaker. Occasionally, glancing over the congregation, he would spy a few of his pals who were sinners. He had been carousing with them during the week – stealing peanuts from the farmers' stacks and usually making a detour by the watermelon patches. Conviction would grip him and he would hang his head in shame.

One day as he talked with some of those same buddies, one of them stated, "Douglas, when it comes to religion I am just as good as you are."

"How is that?" E. J. asked.

"Well," he replied, "you sing in the choir, pray in public and then keep on doing the same things we do. You commit the exact sins the church teaches against."

The hungering young Douglas was smote in his heart as he realized the full impact of what his friend had just told him. But it did not destroy his desire for God. The yearning in his heart for something more continued to linger within him as he grew to be an adult.

During the year of 1913, E. J. married his childhood sweetheart, Eula O'Gwin. The following year, 1914, their home was blessed with the birth of their first child. Thomas O'Guuin was the first of six children born in their home over the years. Following Thomas O'Guuin's birth, three daughters were stillborn. On March 26, 1930, another son Jeff Clark Douglas was born. Although he was born a "blue baby: as were the three daughters, he survived. In 1932 another son was stillborn.

The year 1914 proved to be a happy and eventful year in many ways, for it was in this year that he and his wife heard a message of salvation preached that was to change the entire course of their lives. This message was concerning the "baptism of the Holy Ghost" according to Acts 2:37-40; it was preached by Brother Billy Mills in Beacon, Tennessee, under an old brush arbor.

Dusting off their Bibles, the young couple searched the Scriptures concerning this great subject. After much meditation and study, they realized that this was what their souls had been longing for! Brother Douglas realized this was what he needed to fulfill the mysterious, perplexing, unknown desire, which had lingered within him.

There was much persecution, ridicule, and scornful criticism among the general public concerning the Pentecostals. The mocking, sneering, and insulting remarks by some of their dearest friends cut their hearts to the quick. But they recalled the Bible teaching: "They that live godly shall suffer persecution." Therefore, they proceeded to pray for those who persecuted them and continued seeking for the Holy Ghost.

By this time, what few Pentecostal people there were had erected a small church building in the little community of Beacon. Brother and Sister Douglas began to attend Services. On the night of March 22, 1914, while they were in service, someone tied a half stick of dynamite to a nearby tree, lit the fuse with his cigarette, then proceeded to take his seat inside the crowded church to await the results.

When the explosion came, the whole building trembled. Babies screamed as mothers held them close. Several people left the building and never returned.

After the confusion was over and all those who remained became quiet, Brother Mills calmly stated that the time would come when all those who were not in the ark of safety would flee from God's wrath. The wrath of man was only a small example in comparison to God's fury when He poured out His indignation upon the sinful population of unbelievers.

Seated with head in hands when Brother Mills spoke, Brother Douglas was very discouraged over the outrageous proceedings. But the people began to shout, and Brother Douglas received his infilling of the Spirit. Listen to his own description: "Something seemed to come over me; it engulfed my whole being. The power of God fell on me. Standing to my feet I raised my hands in praise to the Lord. God wonderfully filled me with the Holy Ghost, and I began to speak with other tongues as I had read in Acts 2:4. Great was my rejoicing! Friend, since that moment I can truly state that the longing, yearning desire of my heart has ever been fulfilled."

Two nights later his wife received the same experience. What rejoicing!

In the year of 1915, the call to preach God's Word was so heavy that he surrendered completely to the Lord. He had made many excuses to the Lord, but he remembered that he had promised that he would do anything if he received the Holy Ghost. He dreamed of preaching to great multitudes, and he could visualize numbers of people pleading earnestly to God for salvation. As his soul became more tormented, he slipped away to this secret place of prayer – a little corn crib. It was there he surrendered to God's will, promising to do his best.

After much discussion, he and his trusting wife sold what property they possessed, including their little home.

Combining their resources with that of another minister, Brother Billy Mills, they purchased a tent.

That spring their first destination was the small West Tennessee town of Milan. To their dismay, when they unfolded the tent, they found no ropes or pulleys had been included. They had very little money, but Brother Mills knew the owner of a hardware store and they managed to obtain the missing equipment and put the tent up.

They soon began to realize that some bitter was going to be mixed with the sweet if they were going to preach God's message. The Pentecostal doctrine was completely new to the population of this territory. They had no one there of this belief on whom they could rely for any kind of support. No one offered the hospitality of their home. Brother Mills was fortunate to have a brother who resided in the area, but there was no room in his home for the Douglas family.

Discouraged, Brother Douglas remembered the words of his mother: "Son, I would not advise you to leave home for the ministry. There are very few Pentecostal people. Your support will be very little, and I am afraid you will suffer." However, the zealous young preacher had given her the assurance that he felt God would take care of his family and their needs.

He inquired at a local hotel and found that the rates were one dollar a day for each family member. That was considerable money for a person to earn during those times. They were not required to pay in advance and God did supply their needs by the end of the revival meeting. The young inexperienced preacher stated later that if he had had the money he would have gone home at that point in time and ended his ministry. His faithful wife gave him much encouragement and pleaded with him to stay and rely upon God.

Fifteen people were in the first congregation, but they would take no part in the proceedings. Most of them occupied the back seats and had come to see the "show." The four gospel workers sang, prayed, testified, and Brother Mills preached the sermon. The offering was exactly two nickels.

They saw little results during the four-week campaign. Gradually the crowds increased. Slowly the people began to take part in the services, and the offerings increased. When the little group closed the meeting, they were able to pay their debts. Brother Mills and Brother Douglas had fifteen dollars each.

Their next meeting was located in the small cotton mill town of Trenton, Tennessee. Happily, a Pentecostal man hauled their tent from Milan free. However, by the time they paid expenses plus hired labor for the erection of the tent, it left them practically stranded again. The privation of the previous meeting was only a sample of the difficulties they were to suffer for God's cause in Trenton.

When the four workers opened their first service, not one person would come under the tent. The congregation of about twenty people assembled across the street. In spite of this, the little gospel band again sang, prayed, testified, and preached as if to a large congregation. No sooner was the benediction said than the few quickly left. They dared not tarry long enough to give the workers time to cross the street for a friendly handshake.

Even the friend who had hauled their tent was unexpectedly denied the privilege of attending services for the first few days. This also left them without a place to sleep, for they had planned to stay with him the first night of the revival.

The service over, their efforts seemingly wasted, Brother Douglas and Brother Mills sadly lowered the tent curtains. Where would they sleep that night? It was late and they were not acquainted with anyone in the town. They could not afford a hotel room, and they did not want to ask the hotel manager for credit at that late hour. So they opened their suitcases and spread the clothing on the roughly sawed planks for beds. Their Bibles served as their pillows.

The following morning after prayer, they pooled what little money they had left. Breakfast consisted of a cup of coffee for Brother Mills, who was somewhat older than Brother Douglas, and a glass of milk for little two-year-old Thomas O'Guuin. The others ate cheese and crackers. Lunch for the day was also very meager. However, they were able to acquire a small upstairs room for the women and baby by promising to pay later.

Upon some inquiry they found why the people in the small town were so unfriendly. Not only did they distrust the gospel preachers, they were actually afraid of them. "Preachers were possessed with evil spirits, witchcraft and hypnotism," they thought.

More people attended the second night service. Some ventured to the edge of the tent and a few occupied the back seats. However, when the service was over, they quickly vanished.

The ladies and children went to their room for the night, and the ministers again made their beds on the plank pews.

The third day found the group with very little money. The greater part of that day was spent in meditation and prayer. Somehow they found the courage and made the commitment to continue their evangelistic efforts.

For about a week the preachers continued to sleep on the seats; however, the attendance increased almost to the full capacity of the tent and they received a few meager offerings, including a few coat and shirt buttons, in the collection hat. Somehow they managed to buy food for the women and milk for the baby. Brother Mills and Brother Douglas ate what little they could afford. Although the crowds increased each night, no one invited the preachers to their home.

One day while the hungry preachers were in prayer and meditation, an elderly black lady came to the tent with a tray of fried chicken and hot biscuits saying, "The Lord told me to do this." The preachers quickly called the women and children to enjoy the best meal they had eaten in days.

During the first part of the second week, the campaign began to have visible results. Some people came to the altar, repented, and were gloriously filled with the Holy Ghost; some received healing of different diseases. By the end of the week the altar was filled to overflowing.

However, in the face of all this evidence, several people continued to jeer, criticize, and call them hypnotists. They came to see the "show." What a show produced by God, directed by two of His servants, inspired by His Spirit, with a cast of overjoyed saints speaking in tongues with inspiration from on high.

Out of that revival came two ministers of the gospel, Brother A. N. Graves and Brother Sam Graves. Brother A. N. Graves, who had just left a movie, turned to his friend and stated, "Now, let's go see the other show in town." Before that night was over, he was part of the show itself.

The lighting equipment consisted of the old fashioned, smoky gasoline torches. Seats were made of rough sawmill lumber. After the mayor of the town paid a visit, he had electric lights and fans installed. Straw was spread in the aisles. "Free equipment and volunteer labor. Wonderful," said the Pentecostals.

The congregation swelled to overflowing with many coming from long distances. They came by foot, buggy, wagon, and horseback. The largest crowd was estimated near two thousand. More homes were thrown open to the gospel workers than they could visit. Some of their meals were eaten free of charge at the hotel, and a merchant of the little town gave each of the men a new suit of clothes.

"But the biggest blessing is the many souls that are finding God during this revival," they rejoiced.

The next services Brother Douglas attended were at a camp meeting during the summer of 1915 in Jackson, Tennessee. This was held in a tent which was filled each night and day. Brother H. G. Rodgers, the host pastor, and Brother E. N. Bell conducted the camp. On Sunday night Brother Rodgers estimated the crowd at four thousand.

It was during this camp meeting that Brother and Sister Douglas learned of a new step in obedience they were to take. Brother L. V. Roberts, a noted oneness evangelist of Cincinnati, Ohio, spoke to the Conference. At the close of his first sermon, Brother Bell and Brother Rodgers were baptized in the name of the Lord Jesus in the Forked Deer River. The following Sunday Brother and Sister Douglas, along with Sister Jenny Rodgers and fifty-four others were baptized in the same river in the highest name in heaven and earth – our Lord and Savior Jesus Christ.

Brother Douglas continued to preach, holding meetings in different sections of the country. God blessed greatly by verifying His Word.

Once while conducting a revival near the town of Parsons, Tennessee, a sinner was converted and filled with the Holy Ghost. Rising from the altar, he threw his arms around Brother Douglas. With tears streaming down his face, he confessed that he was guilty of setting off the dynamite on the night that Brother Douglas had received the Holy Ghost. Brother Douglas later baptized Brother Graves in Jesus' name, and as the years passed Brother Graves became a minister and founded a church in the state of Texas.

In the year of 1916, Brother Douglas was called to the state of Missouri where he conducted several revivals, introducing the new revelation of baptism in Jesus' name. In one meeting he was blessed with the privilege of baptizing one hundred and forty-three in His precious name.

It was around this time that he preached a meeting in Parsons, Tennessee. His only convert in that meeting was a teenaged boy named Albert D. Gurley, who later, in 1918 received the Holy Ghost at Mt. Tabor, Tennessee. Brother Gurley became a well-known and effectual minister in the Pentecostal ranks.

As time moved on, some of our ministers, including Brother Douglas, realized the need of a firm footing in organization. In November of 1922, Brother E. J. Douglas, along with another Tennessean, Brother J. C. Brickey, served on the planning committee for a great Bible Conference in Little Rock, Arkansas, where Brother Ralph G. Cook was the host pastor.

In February of 1925, the first general conference and organizational meeting of the Pentecostal Ministerial Alliance was held in Jackson, Tennessee, at the Lexington Avenue Pentecostal Church. This was not intended to be a general church organization but an alliance of ministers; its purpose was to provide for the needs of the ministry; every local church with its pastor was to have sovereign government of its own.

Brother Douglas had the privilege of being a witness to many wonderful demonstrations of God's power concerning healings and miracles. Frequently he visited the sick late at night.

One morning about 1:00 a.m. a farmer came for Brother Douglas to pray for his daughter who was having an epileptic seizure. They traveled several miles in his wagon. When they arrived at the home, the mother was holding a spoon in the unconscious girl's mouth to prevent her from biting her tongue. The girl was very pale and foaming at the mouth. When they prayed in Jesus' name, the girl sat up in bed, raised her hands to heaven and began to speak with other tongues as she was wonderfully filled with the Holy Ghost.

On another occasion their neighbor's daughter became seriously ill. After consultation, two doctors pronounced the case as an excessive amount of infection formed in her side. Since her condition was considered too critical for moving her to the hospital, the doctors set a time for an operation in the home on the following morning. After the doctors left, the family requested that Brother Douglas pray for the girl. The next morning the doctors were very puzzled because they could find nothing wrong with their patient. The infection was gone.

After closing a meeting about twelve miles from his home, Brother Douglas was called to pray for a fellow who was hemorrhaging. In order to pray for the man, Brother Douglas was forced to sacrifice his ride home. After God wonderfully healed the man, the preacher had to walk home through the snow. He cut a hickory stick, ran it through the handle of his suitcase, slung the suitcase over his shoulder, and plodded off through the slippery snow. When he arrived home he was weary in body but happy in his soul. "God does answer prayer," he rejoiced.

Another time, Brother Douglas and a friend walked about ten miles to pray for a fellow minister who was very ill. They walked back afterward. They gave it no thought to walk two, three, or perhaps four miles to a prayer meeting. When it was raining and muddy, they simply donned raincoats and overshoes and went to church.

Somehow they managed to attend services rain or shine, sleet or snow. They walked, traveled by buggy or wagon, and occasionally rode the old gray mule if necessary.

More than once Brother Douglas bought a train ticket and left his wife and children the remaining money. After he had preached a few days and received an offering, he would send more money to his family.

Once while Brother Douglas was doing evangelistic work, his wife was stricken with a slow fever, and he was required to remain at home for several weeks to care for her. He owed a friend ten dollars. Wanting to pay the debt as soon as possible, Brother Douglas prayed, "God, you know I need to pay my debt." A few days later he received a letter from a brother in California with a twenty dollar bill enclosed. God had doubled his request!

One night when service closed, rain poured down. There were no comfortable, dry automobiles to ride home in, so everyone remained in the building for quite a while. "God, please withhold the rain," they prayed and the rain ceased. Brother and Sister Douglas then rode two miles home in a wagon. Just as they stepped inside the door, the rain started again.

During his early ministry, a person's falling prostrate under God's power was a common event. In one service a lady fell, lying prostrate in the service for about two hours. When she was hauled home in a wagon, her parents, being alarmed, called a doctor. He could neither find anything wrong with her, nor could he revive her. Several hours later she awoke, speaking with other tongues as she was wonderfully filled with the Holy Ghost.

During his lifetime, Brother Douglas held many street services in order to reach lost souls who would never darken a church door. He preached in school houses, in homes, on porches, under brush arbors, under trees, in jails, and once in a barn. He accepted every invitation possible as long as he felt that it was God's will to go.

Brother Douglas and Brother A. D. Gurley blessed thousands of people as they traveled to camp meetings, churches and brush arbors around the country. They played their guitars and sang the familiar songs, "50 Miles of Elbow Room" and "The Old Gospel Ship." Many times they received rotten eggs and tomatoes for their singing and preaching, but these "presents" only kindled the fire that was in their souls.

Brother Douglas' preaching ministry spanned forty-four busy years. He pastored and founded several churches in the state of Tennessee, in addition to traveling in evangelistic work from California to East Tennessee, from Michigan to Texas. Many times he filled in pastorates for fellow ministers in time of trouble or ill health. He pastored Lexington Avenue Pentecostal Church in Jackson on three different occasions; he also pastored Beacon Church, Morris Chapel, Enville, Finley, Poplar Corner, Crump, Mt. Tabor, Camden, Trenton, Darden, Midway and other churches in Tennessee.

On November 1, 1954, Brother Douglas was stricken with a severe heart attack. At that time he was living and pastoring in Trenton. After three weeks in the hospital, he was allowed to return home. Although God definitely touched his body, he failed to receive healing. His doctor advised a year's rest.

He stayed at Trenton for several months, but he also bought a retirement home on the Tennessee District Camp Ground at Perryville, Tennessee. After one year of retirement and recuperation, during which time he attended the church in Parsons and wrote a short history of his early ministry, he began again a more active ministry. He conducted weddings, funerals and held small revivals and weekend services in Tennessee, Mississippi and Missouri.

While Brother Douglas was preaching a revival for Brother A. N. Graves in the spring of 1957, his wife slipped on a rug in the home of their son Jeff. The fall broke her hip. She was confined to bed until her death two months later.

After his wife's death, Brother Douglas sold his home on the camp grounds and moved to Parsons, Tennessee where he later met and married a widow, Mrs. Carrie Pierce.

Again he accepted the pastorate of the Mt. Tabor Church and became happily engaged in pastoral work.

On the Sunday night before Labor Day, September 6, 1959, Brother Douglas was scheduled to preach at the Parsons Church for the pastor, Brother R. B. Boyd. Requests were turned in for him to sing "50 Miles of Elbow Room" and "The Old Gospel Ship." His son and daughter-in-law, Jeff and Frances, were there, and Jeff played for his father. After singing "The Old Gospel Ship," Brother Douglas made the statement, "I'll soon be gone and I wonder who will sing this song when I am gone."

There was a request made for Brother Douglas and his son and daughter-in-law to sing "It is No Secret What God Can Do" before the message. Before they rose to sing, Brother Douglas turned to Jeff. "I am very hot and I need to rest before I preach. You and Frances sing."

While they were singing, Brother Douglas moved down in the audience to sit by an open window. He turned to the man sitting next to him, and then got up to go out. With the help of his friend, he made it to the back of the church where he collapsed and died of a heart attack.

Brother Douglas' funeral was conducted by Brother W. M Greer, with the assistance of Brother A. N. Graves and Brother A. D. Gurley, in the Parsons Church. Sister Berthal

Crossno, a lady pioneer Pentecostal preacher who was converted under Brother Douglas" early ministry, sang.

In Brother Douglas' little book entitled, *My Early Ministry*, he wrote the following statement to younger ministers: "We older ministers have paved the road, but our day is almost spent. God wishes His work to be carried on. The responsibility of lost souls lies on your shoulders. Do your share."

Sister Flatt, son Owner, Sister Mollie Edwards of Finley, Tennessee, Brother Nelson Flatt, Brother E. J. Douglass, Brother Kerley. Around fifty received the Holy Ghost in this revival!

Brother Douglas and Bro. Odell Cagle in a vineyard.

Brother and Sister E. J. Douglas standing here beside their automobile.

JAMES ELMER ROSS
By Mary Jackson
Information from Jan Johnson, granddaughter

James Elmer Ross was born in rural Madison County near Pinson, Tennessee in June of 1889. His mother died when he was only four years old. His many stepmothers were not pleasant experiences, and he left home at an early age.

James met and married Emma Dyer in September 1908. To this union was added a son, Clifford, in 1910. Seven years later their happiness was increased when in 1917 their daughter, Ruth, was born. But this double joy of two children ended in 1920 when Clifford died at the age of ten. Another daughter, Sue, was born in March of 1921. The fourth child -- a son, Jimmy -- was born in 1924.

Due to the unpleasant home life in James' childhood, he did not attend public school. When he and Emma married, he could neither read nor write. Emma became not only his helpmate, but his teacher also. Her expertise as a teacher was manifested in her student. James became a skilled carpenter and could not only read blueprints but was able to figure materials required for building. By the time he began his ministry as a preacher, he was very affluent in reading the scriptures.

The exact date of Brother Ross' dedication to God is not known, but he was saved under the ministry of Brother H. G. Rodgers and his daughter, Ethel, in Jackson, Tennessee. When Brother E. N. Bell came to Jackson with the revelation of Jesus' Name baptism, he was probably among the large number baptized in Jesus' Name by Brother Bell in the Forked Deer River in 1916. At that time his very close friend and co-worker, Brother C. M. Goff, was baptized and also Brother H. G. Rodgers, Brother E. J. Douglas and over 50 others. Brother Ross very soon acknowledged his call to the ministry, and he and Brother Goff, who lived next door, held revivals together. They also worked together in the carpentry business.

Brother Ross was a very tender hearted man. It has been said that when his daughter Ruth and her friend, Geneva, would play their duet on the piano, he would sit and weep. He was so moved by love and the Spirit. He was a kind and loving husband and father.

His first pastorate was in Truman, Arkansas. Later he pastored in Ridgely, Tennessee; Dyersburg, Tennessee; twice in Camden, Tennessee, and he also served the Lexington Avenue Church in Jackson, Tennessee at two different times.

Brother Ross was well known as an expert carpenter as well as a minister. Brother W. M. Greer, pastor of the Bemis Pentecostal Church, had a vision of enlarging the church auditorium, adding a prayer room and another Sunday School wing. He immediately thought of Brother Ross to oversee this project. Shortly after the District Conference at Bemis in April 1949, Brother Greer contacted Brother Ross. He and Sister Ross moved into the evangelists' quarters at the church, and he began work on the building. Brother Ross helped design and re-arrange the auditorium to its present size. A prayer room was added behind the auditorium and connected to a new two-story Sunday School addition.

The work at the Bemis Church was completed in December 1949 and Brother Ross was elected pastor for the second time at the Lexington Avenue Pentecostal Church in Jackson. When he left the Jackson church, he was elected pastor at the Camden church. While there, he was appointed to be one of the first presbyters of the newly formed Tennessee District of the United Pentecostal Church, Inc. Brother W. M. Greer, the Superintendent of the District, felt it would be good to divide the district into three sections and Brother Ross and Brother E. J. Douglas were appointed presbyters of the Central Section.

The skill of Brother Ross was well known by this time and he and Sister Ross moved to Tupelo, Mississippi where he helped with the construction of Tupelo Children's Mansion. The officials of the United Pentecostal Church, Inc. had learned of Brother Ross and his expertise in building, and they called him to St. Louis, Missouri to help build the second Headquarters building.

Sadness was a part of his life as well as blessings. Not only did he and Sister Ross lose their first son, Clifford, at a young age, but their baby boy, Jimmy, only lived to be forty years old. He died in 1964. Their daughter Ruth died in 1966. They retired to Memphis, Tennessee after a profitable ministry. Here they were close to their daughters, Sue and Ruth, before Ruth's death. He was a faithful member of the Calvary United Pentecostal Church in Memphis until his death in 1969. Sister Ross was still living in Memphis at the time of her death in 1975.

J.E. Ross Baptizing

J. W. WALLACE
By Mrs. Glenn C. Wallace, daughter-in-law

James Welles Wallace was born in rural Decatur County, Tennessee on April 1, 1890. In 1918, a little-known oneness Pentecostal minister, Brother Kennedy, built a brush arbor in Decatur County and held a revival meeting. Both J. W. and his wife, Allie, received the Holy Ghost. They gladly heard the Word and accepted the Oneness message.

In 1922, Brother and Sister Wallace moved their family of three boys, Cleatus, Onell (J.O.) and Glenn and a daughter, Naomi, to Bemis, Tennessee. The family soon became active in the Bemis Pentecostal Church. In November 1925, God blessed their home with another daughter, Vaughncile (Bonnie). While in Bemis, Brother Wallace was called into the ministry. He served as Assistant Pastor to Brother A. D. Gurley from 1923 until 1937. Brother Wallace was ordained in Jackson, Tennessee on March 7, 1935. During the time he served as Assistant Pastor, he built a church in Chester County in the Pleasant Ridge Community. He pastored the Bemis Pentecostal Church in 1939-1940.

Brother Wallace had an intense desire to accomplish more for the Lord after reaching the age of 50 years than he had prior. In 1941, he felt a definite call to start a church in Nashville and to establish churches east of the Tennessee River. He moved his family to Nashville and began holding cottage meetings. Property was purchased on the corner of 51st and Delaware Avenue. A tent was pitched and the first revival was held in May of 1941. A basement church was built and paid for during the difficult years of World War II. The auditorium was completed and dedicated in February, 1948. Brother A. D. Gurley was the guest speaker. Brother M. H. Hansford conducted the first revival meeting in the new auditorium.

During the growth of the West Nashville Pentecostal Church (now First UPC) Brother Wallace, along with his son, Rev. J. O. and daughter-in-law, Mary, was responsible for the founding of the Goodlettsville Pentecostal Church and the Woodbine Pentecostal Church (Now Christ Church-Pentecostal). Brother Wallace later started the church in Oak Ridge, Tennessee where he purchased two acres of land for the church site.

Brother Wallace served as a member of the District Board of the Southern District and as an original member of the Tennessee District Board of the U.P.C.I. He was a member of the Board of Directors of the Tupelo Bible Institute for a period of over five years. Brother Wallace was also Chairman of the Board of Directors.

In 1951, while an active member of the Tennessee District Board, Brother Wallace was selected as the builder for the Tennessee District Campground at Perryville. He drew the plans for the first building, the dining hall and kitchen. The large tabernacle soon followed.

In 1957, the West Nashville Church had a note burning service and a special day honoring Brother and Sister

Wallace for their faithful labors which brought about the fulfillment of a vision from cottage prayer meetings to a beautiful debt-free church in just 16 years.

A heart condition forced Brother Wallace to retire from full-time ministry about three years prior to his death on January 18, 1959.

"Blessed are the dead which die in the Lord from henceforth; yea, saith the Spirit, that they may rest from their labours; and their works do follow them." (Rev. 14:13) Brother Wallace's sacrificial life produced fruit that survived even death.

(Above) Rev. & Mrs. J. W. Wallace
(Right) The Wallace Family at Bemis Tennessee about 1940.

(Above) First UPC Sunday School in Nashville, 1941
(Left) "Go East, older man, go East!"

O. W. WILLIAMS
Autobiography

I was born in the State of Tennessee on May 3, 1919 and continued to reside there for the next thirty-four years. My wife was born on January 29, 1920. Her maiden name was Violet Lynch, and she is now 79 years old. By the grace of God, we had three lovely children born into our family. Virginia who was the oldest is no longer with us. She held a prestigious position as assistant principal at the Humble School, but cancer took her from us about four years ago. We do miss her, but thank God for her dedication. Our second child is Laverne Stanton Williams, who has now excelled to the position of a Legal Secretary in Dallas, Texas. Then of course there is my baby daughter, whose name is now Demi Wagner. She teaches school in a small town called Colmesneil. So those are my children. My dad and my mother were old frontier folks. In fact, Dad was born in 1872 and Mom was born in 1879. Mother passed away in 1951 and Dad in 1962. There were fourteen children born of that union. Only ten matured to adulthood, while the other four died prematurely, either at birth or shortly thereafter. So we had quite a large family, but it was a pleasure to be a rural family on a hillside in Tennessee. I am the thirteenth of fourteen children.

Therefore, most of my siblings are passed away, but we still thank God everyday for the fellowship we enjoyed and the many joyous days we walked together.

There were several great men of God who played extremely significant roles in the shaping and molding of my ministry and my life. For instance, my original mentor was Brother Johnny Stubblefield from Jackson, Tennessee. He was an evangelist, whom I first encountered at a little country schoolhouse on what we then called Cane Creek in middle Tennessee. He stayed and preached a revival for us for one week while receiving approximately $2.50 for his work during that week. It was here that the Lord Jesus touched my soul and I knelt there at the little rise where the teachers directed the students in their studies and gave my heart to the Lord Jesus Christ. It was a beautiful experience – weeping, worshipping, and confessing my sins. After I had repented, Brother Stubblefield took me down to old Cane Creek under the beautiful willow trees where the water was gently and peacefully flowing over the smooth rocks that had for years lay there in the busy currents of that celestial stream, and he buried me in water baptism in the the lovely name of the Lord Jesus Christ for the remission of my sins.

After this, I continued to study and began attending a community service, held each Sunday at another church we called Upper Sinking. This too was a little schoolhouse. It was here that while the minister was so powerfully preaching the word of the Lord, the awesome and overwhelming power of God fell on me, and I was immediately consumed with the power of the Holy Ghost, so much so, that I fell to the ground where I lay speaking in other tongues as the Spirit gave the utterance for some four hours before I was taken home.

From my school there, I transferred to Nashville, and when I completed my schooling there, I moved to Memphis where I became a member of the First Pentecostal Church as well as a pupil under Brother E. E. McNatt's ministry. During the time of my apprenticeship to Brother McNatt, I enjoyed several nights, sometimes 'til two or three o'clock in the morning, in which he sacrificed his precious time and energy instructing me in the Word of the Lord. He taught me how to live and how to be loyal, faithful, and dedicated and what it means to be completely consecrated to God. This continued for quite some time, and as I was searching for my calling with Brother McNatt, I learned the meaning of true conviction. When we were attending the old Pickwick Lake Camp Meeting in Iuka, Mississippi, I held a brief conversation with Brother A. D. Gurley who was our District Superintendent at the time. During this particular meeting, I made the comment to Brother Gurley that I had asked God to talk to me and tell me personally that he wanted me to preach. Brother Gurley, in the nicest manner possible, asked me if I thought my demands were a little bit strong. And since I knew my demands were too strong, I answered, "Yes, Brother Gurley, I suppose they are." And within an hour of that conversation I remember feeling so convicted that I had demanded anything of the Lord, thereby realizing my place in Christ's kingdom was not to give decree, but rather to become subjected to God's authority and His divine will and purpose for my life. As a result of my hasty desire, I knelt just above old Pickwick Lake beside an old crooked tree. That was in 1943 and at that old crooked tree, I told the Lord Jesus that I would do whatever he wanted me to do, and I would do it to the best of my ability. It was here that I began my ministry and continued in Tennessee for the next decade. In 1953 I felt to change directions in my ministry and relocate to Texas.

Having completed my schooling in Nashville, I had moved to Memphis to become employed with Fisher Memphis Aircraft Division. During my time with this illustrious position, my pastor, Brother McNatt began to guide and direct my path in the Lord and in the study of the Word, the Bible. Brother McNatt left a lasting impression upon my life which can be felt in my ministry to this very day. I will never forget the great teaching and direction that he so unselfishly poured into my life and my ministry.

Brother A. D. Gurley was my District Superintendent at that time. Brother W. M. Greer and Brother McNatt served as Presbyters in the Southeastern District of The Pentecostal Church, Inc. All of this began to aid me in my endeavor to locate a place to preach, thus marking the beginning of the fulfilling of God's purpose for my life. At this time, I had never held a revival. I had never even been out anywhere to preach. So, with that in mind, you can envision the picture of inexperience that my mentors had to work with as far as "selling" my ability, so to speak, to surrounding churches and ministers. However, Brother J. H. Austin was kind enough to take me in for a two-week revival. The Lord richly blessed the preached Word of God and there were some baptized in the Holy Ghost. Now when that revival was finished, I moved on to Nashville, Tennessee where Brother J. W. Wallace was the pastor of the church which was located at 51st and Delaware. We preached for two weeks there and Brother Wallace and the people there were so very kind and hospitable. We greatly enjoyed ourselves there. Next, my evangelistic ministry led me to Sister Lela Holland's church in Hohenwald, Tennessee. Sister Holland was so gracious in opening her church to me and granting to me every privilege that any evangelist could ever expect to receive. In that church the Lord Jesus gave me one of the greatest revivals I suppose I had seen up to that point.

There were sixteen who received the gift of the Holy Ghost with the evidence of speaking in other tongues. During this time, we chose to stay in constant revival seven nights a week, feeling that if we missed a night, it may well adversely affect our success in the altars. With that in mind, we preached every night of the week, but we believed that it did not matter to what degree God was blessing a church, a revival must cease at the two-week point, so we left Hohenwald and began to move into other areas, evangelizing.

Then in 1945, Brother Gurley, Brother Greer and Brother McNatt took me down to Ridgely, Tennessee where they had found a church which had been vacated for quite some time. Upon receiving the approval of the brethren, Brother Greer purchased that church with funds that were made available to him through one of his good friends, and this incident became the beginning of my pastoral responsibilities. We proceeded to move into the church in February. I sold my wife's cook stove for $35.00 so that we would have enough money to move and she still tells me about having to move there in an old cattle trailer that still had woodchips in the bed of it. Although we faced many hardships, we enjoyed our ten years at that location. In the meantime, there was a Church of God building in Tiptonville, Tennessee and we managed to purchase it and began a congregation at that location after being in Ridgely only six years. Near the end of our time in Ridgely, the Lord had begun to deal with me about a little town of about 8000 people only 31 miles away called Union City. Although I had attempted to persuade several other men in the ministry to take on that burden with my assisting them, I could find no one. And of course this was because it was a burden God had given me and no one else at that time. Simply put, it was my responsibility. As a result of the burden God had given me for this city, we proceeded to foster a work in Union City, and naturally God greatly honored our obedience. Initially, we did not have one member to preach to. So I mortgaged my automobile for $1,000 and borrowed $1,000 on my name and bought a nice lot there in Union City. Then, we began planning to build a church only to realize that there were no finances available to build anything. However, I did have a friend in Ridgely by the name of Damon Headon, who was a very wealthy man and whose face I saw in a vision one morning while I was praying. I then got up and informed my wife that I was going to Ridgely to speak with Damon Headon, because I felt as though the Lord had ordained that I go ask him about furnishing the lumber needed to construct the church in Union City. When I arrived at his big sawmill plant, I found that he was out in the yard of his mill, so I walked up to him and said, "Mr. Headon, I want to build a church in Union City, but I don't have any money. I just wondered if there would be a possibility of you furnishing the lumber and let me build it and allow me to pay for it by the month or however." And of course he talked loudly and said, "Preacher! I'll take everyone of my trucks and put every stick of lumber you need over there to build that church, and when I have finished putting it on the ground for you, I'll write you a bill for it all and give you fifty percent off the total cost." That's exactly what he did. He sent five truck loads of lumber over there to build that church, and today, to the best of my knowledge, Ridgely, Tiptonville and Union City all three have full-time pastors.

Now in the midst of all my business in Tennessee, I felt a call to minister in Texas. We'll discuss that ministry more in depth a little later. First, let me tell you about my being elected Youth Director in the Southern District of the United Pentecostal Church after the merger in 1945. This occurred while I was yet pastoring at Ridgely. I filled this position for a couple of years and was also elected one year to fill the Home Missions Director's position. Brother H. A. Goss was attending the conference of the old Southern District of Tennessee, Mississippi and Alabama at that time. It was April 1949 that the Southern District was divided and Tennessee became a separate district. While Brother Goss was there, the brethren moved to elect me as a presbyter in the District of Tennessee. However, I was only twenty-nine years old at the time, and the district had a standing regulation stating that all presbyters must be at least age thirty or above to fill that position. Brother Goss waived this ruling since I would be thirty in just one month, thereby allowing me to be voted onto the board of Presbyters for the District of Tennessee. Brother Greer was our District Superintendent and was a very fine, aggressive man in the ministry and work that came with his position.

Let it be said that my memory has not yet failed me, and my respect is still very high for the brethren and the leadership and all the children of God of the State of Tennessee. To be completely honest with you, I am still in my heart a Tennessean, a fellow brother of that state which was established in the Gospel of Jesus Christ.

At this time I would like to briefly speak on events surrounding my experiences in the State of Texas. After my time in Tennessee was over, I was elected to pastor a church in Kilgore, Texas where I labored for nearly six years. After that a church in Houston, Texas elected me as their pastor, and I was there for nearly fourteen years. It was there that we built a church which seated close to 1100 people. It was at this time, that the good people of Texas elected me to the highly esteemed office of District Superintendent. I held that position for quite a few years, and it was under my direction that we built perhaps the largest tabernacle in Pentecost at that time, and it was located on the campground.

After being elected three times to the office of District Superintendent, I informed my dear brethren that I wished to continue my ministry as a pastor. I did so in Lufkin, Texas and continued pastoring there for nearly eighteen years.

This year is now 1999, and five years ago I trained a young man that had worked with me loyally and had dedicated his life so beautifully to God. This young man is Leon Wallace. Soon after, I felt that he was ready, and I asked the church to elect him to the pastoral position, and thankfully they agreed. Now Brother Wallace has been here five years, and he is doing a very fine job. I'm still preaching all over the area. I just recently had my 80th birthday, and everything is going smoothly. As always, God has been great to us. My wife and I have had a wonderful time in the ministry. I am now in my 57th year in the ministry of the Gospel of Jesus Christ, and it just gets sweeter and sweeter every day.

May God richly bless you, and we Salute the Tennessee District!

O. W. Williams, former member of the Tennessee District Board, founder of the Union City First UPC, former District Superintendent of the Texas District, pictured here with Sister Williams

A. D. Gurley, District Superintendent of the Southeastern District of the Pentecostal Church, Incorporated, along with O. W. Williams beside a vintage automobile.

The O. W. Williams Family: Demi, LaVerne, Virginia, Wife, Violet, and O. W. Williams.

CLOVIS TURNBOW
By Harold Jaco, Jr.

Clovis Turnbow was born on August 15, 1917 in Lewis County, Tennessee. His parents were the late Tommy and Carrie Lindsey Turnbow. They were good, honest people who worked hard at farming. His mother was an English teacher in the county school and attended the Church of Christ in their community. His father was Presbyterian in belief but rarely went to church. Clovis had four brothers: Leland, Ward, Wilton and James; and three sisters: Lockye, Esther and Inerea.

Young Clovis, like his dad, did not attend church regularly. He helped on the family farm until he was called into service in the U. S. Army during World War II. Not only Clovis but two of his brothers, Leland and Ward, were in the Army. They left home at different times but during the war, Clovis and Leland met unexpectedly in Europe. This was a very exciting experience for them.

After he returned from the war, Clovis married Lila Sharp. But shortly after their daughter, Laverne, was born, Clovis and Lila separated. Neither wanted a divorce, so for years they each lived their own lives. Many years later, Clovis and Lila divorced.

In 1940, Sister Lela Holland was conducting services in Lewis County near Hohenwald, Tennessee. It was in that meeting that Clovis Turnbow came into contact with Jesus Christ, and it changed the life of this twenty-three year old young man.

After a few years of growing in his walk with the Lord in the local church, Clovis went to Tupelo, Mississippi to attend the Pentecostal Bible Institute at 405 Clayton Avenue. He was dedicated and committed to developing his life into the ministry. In 1949 he graduated from the Bible school.

Later in 1949, Brother Turnbow accepted his first pastorate at the Bethel Springs Pentecostal Church. He served there for a few years, reaching into the community with his preaching, visiting, and outstanding life of prayer.

Tennessee District United Pentecostal Church Annual Conference in Dyersburg, Tennessee, was a "red letter" time for Brother Turnbow. On April 3, 1952, under the hand and prayers of District Superintendent W. M. Greer and the brethren of the District Board, Brother Clovis Turnbow was ordained into the ministry. Having received this full credential, he felt prepared to proceed further with his ministry.

From Bethel Springs, Brother Turnbow went to Blue Goose (then known as the Spring Hill Pentecostal Church) and preached there. The Arlon Anderson family as well as the Cagles, and others were a part of that congregation and enjoyed the ministry of this man of God who led with a prayerful, but gentle hand. It was under his leadership that the church was moved from the south side of Highway 412 (then known as Highway 29 (in the Spring Hill community to the north side of the highway and into the Blue Goose Community. The church name was changed to the Blue Goose Pentecostal Church and a small building was constructed on land donated by Brother Arlon Anderson.

After a while, though, the call of God caused Brother Turnbow to move on.

The next stop on his way was the First Pentecostal Church of Savannah. Brother Turnbow served as pastor to the Harwell family, the DeBerry family and many others. His influence on the life of a young man named Sammy Chessor helped direct him into the ministry. Many others went out into the ministry from the able leadership of this pastor.

As a single man, Brother Turnbow was very thankful for his spinster sister, Sister Esther Turnbow, who worked faithfully with him in the churches he pastored. She was a valuable asset to his ministry. While pastoring at the Beacon Junction Pentecostal Church (now Beacon United Pentecostal Church), Sister Esther passed away. He was so moved by the loss of his faithful supporter, that he resigned the church at Beacon and stepped out into an evangelistic ministry for a number of years.

Brother Turnbow evangelized until 1975. During this time, he met and was married to Sister Inez Hill of Dyersburg, Tennessee. The new Sister Turnbow became a great asset to his ministry and provided him with the help and support he needed on the home front.

In 1975, Brother Turnbow accepted the call to the Bruceton United Pentecostal Church where he served as pastor until 1978 when his health began to break. That year he had heart surgery in an attempt to correct coronary disease. But this surgery was only marginally successful. It left this conscientious man of God without the strength to carry out his pastoral ministry at Bruceton. Because he was unable to do what he felt needed to be done for the church, he resigned as pastor.

In 1980, the Turnbow's moved to Chicago, Illinois to live near family and receive the help and support they needed at the time. During this time, Brother Turnbow served as assistant pastor to Brother Rick Wyser for two years.

When they felt to move back to the south, they returned to Dyersburg, Tennessee to live in the house near Newbern, Tennessee which Sister Turnbow owned before they were married. The Turnbows attended the First United Pentecostal Church in Dyersburg, sitting under the ministry of Brother Eric McDougal. During this time, with failing health, Brother Turnbow continued to exercise his ministry of prayer and intercession.

Among the many special services Brother Turnbow performed in the Tennessee District of the United Pentecostal Church, he was the first elected Director of Home Missions. In 1954, the district felt the need to reach out and promote the building of new churches across the state and Brother Turnbow was elected to lead this endeavour. He was a member of the District Board from 1955 to 1959. This is the highest executive body of the church in the Tennessee District.

In 1990, when death began to seize upon the life of this preacher of the Gospel, his wife relates that he turned to her, looking full into her face as though he were going to tell her something. However, instead of explaining to her what he wanted to say in English, he spoke in tongues for some thirty minutes before slipping into a coma, never to awaken again in this world.

Sister Inez Turnbow speaks of his prayer life with great reverence. She indicated that she had never seen anyone who prayed so much nor so effectively as this great man of God. In grieving his passing, even nine years later, she asks for the prayers of her friends and loved ones because she can no longer count on his prayers to help her through.

Brother Turnbow and his Sister, Esther, who was a faithful helper in his ministry for many years.

Brother Turnbow when he was serving as Tennessee District Home Missions Secretary.

A PROMISE FROM GOD
By Lela Holland

It was in the year 1913 that a baby girl who was given the name Lela Mae came to live in the home of Noah and Lillie Chumney. They were God fearing, honest, hard-working parents. This was before the days of modern conveniences. Water was either brought from a spring or drawn up from a well. Wash day was an all-day affair with clothes being scrubbed on a rub board, boiled in a huge black pot, and hung on a line to dry. People earned their living in the cotton and corn fields. It was hard work, but safe. There were no automobiles; I never saw one until I was about six years old. So you see, children's minds could grow and expand in God's beautiful world.

I went to one-room country schools where the Bible was read and prayer offered every morning. I really desired to get a high school education, but it didn't seem possible as there were no school buses in those days. God in His great plan made a way, although not an easy one, but I did make it! It was while I was away at school that I went to a Holiness Church revival and received the great experience that changed my life and my future. Thank God! Space prohibits my relating how the Lord confirmed to me that He would give the grace and power needed to perform His ministry in my life. And He has done just that!

From brush arbors, schoolhouses, abandoned church houses, etc. the Lord saw that "two would be better than one" in the ministry. So in March of 1934 while in a revival at Adamsville, Tennessee some people from Beauty Hill Pentecostal Church visited the revival on Easter Sunday. A young man by the name of Carlos Holland was included in the group. We were introduced and from there our interest and care for one another progressed. We were married on December 1, 1934.

Our ministry has not been one of glamour or heralded as a big success, but we've tried to find places to work and things to do that maybe looked unattractive or plain too hard work for some. My partner has been a stable, caring person who has added many, many more points to our ministry. We worked in different places in West Tennessee before beginning our ministry in Lewis County, Tennessee in the year of 1939. The ministry God gave to us was definitely not a lucrative one, moneywise. Brother Holland has definitely been the provider.

In October of 1941, we moved to Lewis County not knowing how God would provide. It was really a test of our faith, but we knew it was God's plan. Revival and miracles like we had never seen came to pass, including a child paralyzed from the waist down being completely and gloriously healed. Many people were being saved. In February of 1942, a bus load of people including twenty-seven converts to be baptized were taken to Corinth, Mississippi for Rev. A. D. Gurley, our Superintendent, to baptize.

Brother Gurley came in May of 1942 to the little country church and raised $500 in pledges to purchase a lot in Hohenwald on which to build a church. Small amount of money? Yes, but that was depression times. One lady sold her piano to get her pledge. How did we live? Only God knows! Brother Holland and another man in the church skinned a mule that had died and sold the hide for $10. On another occasion they dug a well for $15. All this hurt my dear husband's pride, for he had always desired to be a good provider. God had us in a training program. We were desperately trying to pass the test.

The pledges came in, and a beautiful lot was purchased on which the First Pentecostal Church is located. Brother A. D. Gurley helped us secure a loan from someone he knew in the amount of $3,000. Knowing we had to spend wisely, Brother Holland laid the blocks for $1 (one dollar) per day.

In August of that year, a tent was pitched on the lot with Brother Gurley again being the evangelist. My what a revival! Dozens were converted, and there were Holy Ghost infillings and baptizings nearly every day. We regretted that the evangelist had to endure our primitive lifestyle conveniences with no indoor plumbing or bathroom facilities, but he made us feel good that we were doing our best for him and for God's kingdom.

The church grew from 100 in Sunday School to the point that more facilities had to be added. In 1944, an addition was added which provided adequate space for growth. In the late 1940's the attendance had reached 135 or more. The good Lord had provided my husband with a nice job in the local General Shoe plant. He had proven his worth and was now a supervisor there.

We had some wonderful years in the Hohenwald Pentecostal Church. Many had come to God. Eight ministers who had received the Holy Ghost during this period of time were now on the field. Our family had grown up there. But in 1950, we moved on and left the precious fruit God had given us in other hands. Incidentally, my top salary while there was thirty-five ($35) dollars per week.

We worked in Linden for two years. Brother W. M. Greer asked us about starting a work in Lexington, Tennessee. We accepted the challenge. In August of 1952, Brother E. E. McNatt preached a tent revival on the beautiful lots where the present church is located. From there we moved to the National Guard building. We had 19 in Sunday School on our first Sunday. The interest grew, and on December 1, 1952, a basement church had been completed, and we moved in. It was such a pleasure to work with those wonderful people for five years. Our four children had grown up and were such a wonderful help. When we were ready to leave the church, it had grown in attendance to seventy-five. Those precious people asked us to get the pastor. We left the church in the capable hands of Brother W. D. McCollum. It was a wonderful church with wonderful people!

Due to a reaction from a serious surgery, my voice failed, and I could not minister for several years. A place in the Lewis County School System opened, and I had the privilege of teaching with a black lady in the formative years of school integration. Lewis County was chosen as a pilot kindergarten school. It was challenging, but rewarding. I was waiting, hoping that sometime I could minister and sing again. Finally, it came! Brother Escar Tharp asked us to help him at the Mt. Zion Pentecostal Church. We did, and again my "church-building" husband had the privilege of overseeing the building of a beautiful sanctuary at Mt. Zion.

In closing, allow me to add just a line of information regarding the wonderful people we've been privileged to work with these many years. At the Tennessee Spring

Conference in 1934 when Brother W. E. Kidson was General Secretary of the Pentecostal Church, Inc., I was approved for my first local license.

When I married and moved to a different area, I found these people were working with the Church of the Lord Jesus Christ. Brother T. C. Montgomery was the General Superintendent. He later affiliated with the United Pentecostal Church and was the founder of the Tupelo Children's Mansion. In 1935 we were asked to go to East Tennessee to work in Cleveland and the surrounding area. I was ordained for this work. We went on up into the mountains. It was different, but we had some great experiences.

When we returned, it was our desire to work with the people we had known in the beginning. It was in 1945 that the merger had taken place, and it was now the United Pentecostal Church. At my request, I was again sent forth by the laying on of hands, and was ordained into the United Pentecostal Church fellowship in March of 1946.

My ordination license hangs on the wall signed by Brother H. A. Goss, General Superintendent; Brother W. T. Witherspoon, Assistant General Superintendent and Brother A. D. Gurley, District Superintendent. I had rather my life be taken than I should ever bring a reproach on a cause I so dearly love.

In April 1954, at the Conference of the Tennessee District, Brother W. M. Greer, District Superintendent, organized the Ladies Auxiliary. He asked me to serve as the first president of this department. Sister Berthal Crossno was to serve with me as secretary. Our first task was to provide food and get together equipment for the kitchen at the camp ground. I traveled many miles to different churches to organize and set in order Ladies Auxiliary groups. It was a joy to work with the wonderful ladies of the district, for four years, but my burden was to spend more time in preaching. I resigned the leadership of the Ladies Auxiliary in April 1958.

Now to end the treatise ... Brother Holland and I are both retired now, but there's a "calling" that will never be stilled – and a "promise from God" that will always last. I suppose I feel somewhat like the old retired horse that had raced across the town pulling the fire wagon. This had been his life so long that when the fire whistle sounded, he immediately placed himself in position to "take off." Years passed, more modern equipment was now being used, and "Old Dobbin" was given the privilege to take it easy at pasture. It didn't work that way! When the whistle blew, he raced to the barn to be harnessed and race to the fire!

I realize that physically our strength and motivation have somewhat diminished, "but not the call!" "For the gifts and calling of God are without repentance." Romans 11:29. "For all the promises of God in Him are yea; and in Him amen, unto the glory of God by us." II Corinthians 1:20.

The Carlos Holland Family

First Pentecostal Church of Hohenwald, pastored by Lela Holland

Brother and Sister Carlos Holland

Young Preacher Lady
Lela Holland

BERTHAL JONES CROSSNO
By Wayne Chester

Sorghum and chert gravel were two things Benton County, Tennessee, became famous for, but on May 5, 1911, an event happened that has affected Benton County and surrounding counties in a more lasting way.

Born to John Robert Jones and Laura Pierce Jones was a baby girl, whom they named Berthal Mae Jones. This was by no means their only child as Berthal was one of eight children.

"Children, get the wood in and get all the chores done. We're going to church tonight. I hear they are having a good revival up at Cowells Chapel Methodist Church," Berthal's mother told her children.

Berthal was excited. She liked to go to church. The Jones children often played church in their playhouses that they made in the edge of the woods. They all would sing, and someone would preach. Although they started out playing, many times a spirit of genuine worship developed and God began to bless the children. They would sometimes weep before the Lord.

"Now, you children be good and pay attention to what that preacher has to say," Mother admonished them. "Church is no place to play."

Berthal was very attentive, and when the evangelist gave the altar call, conviction gripped her heart. At the age of eleven, Berthal made her way to the front of the church and repented of her sins.

"Hey, Momma," cried Aaron, one of Berthal's older brothers, "We were up in the south end of the county last night, and they were having one of those "holy roller" meetings. I have never seen anything like that before. It sure looked like they were enjoying themselves. People were shouting and praising God and some lady threw her hands up and began to speak in a language that I have never heard." Berthal had not heard anything like this before. How she would like to go and see something like this!

At the supper table that night, John Robert, Berthal's daddy, said, "I would like to go to one of those holiness services. I'll tell you what we'll do: I'll quit a little early tomorrow, and we'll go. All of you children get all your work done early.

Berthal was excited! "I can't wait to see what goes on," she thought to herself.

The next evening, John Robert hitched up the mules to the old steel rim wagon and loaded the family. Berthal's mother sat with her mother on the springboard seat while the children sat on some quilts in the bed of the wagon. The jostling often gave Berthal a side ache, but she enjoyed the wagon ride anyway. Her mother always put in some extra quilts to cover up on the way home from church as the air was often cool at night.

Brother William Boyd and Brother C. M. Goff were in charge of the revival that was being held at Smith Grove School about six miles south of Camden, Tennessee.

Berthal watched everything that went on in the service. "My, this is sure different from the services at Cowells Chapel," she thought to herself. This was Berthal's first encounter with Pentecost. As the old wagon rumbled its way back home, Berthal pondered the things she had seen and heard in her heart.

In 1924, Brother J. C. Brickey came to Old Depot, a little community near Camden, Tennessee, and pitched a tent and began to preach the Word of God with great power and anointing.

The Jones family liked what they had felt at the revival at Smith Grove School, so they started attending the tent meeting. God began to talk to their hearts. They began to realize that there was a deeper experience for them than what they had felt thus far. Several members of the Jones' family came to know God in the power of the Holy Ghost.

There still was no church in Camden that preached the full plan of salvation. The closest church was about six miles away. And with no way to travel except by wagon, the Jones family did not get to attend church on a regular basis. However, they began to have cottage prayer meetings. This proved to be a great blessing to them.

Berthal was one of the more stubborn children of the family. It took her nearly three years to get her fleshly nature under control and in subjection to God.

A revival was announced at Flowers Chapel Pentecostal Church. The Jones family was excited. It was a long way to travel by wagon, but they wanted to attend as many services as possible.

On one particular night of the revival, September 21, 1927, Berthal made her way down to the front of the church when the altar call was given, and she began to seek the Lord with all her heart. The power of God came upon her and she spoke a few words in other tongues as the Spirit gave the utterance. There was much rejoicing that night in that service.

But the next morning, Berthal had some doubts. She was not sure that she had received the Holy Ghost.

"Berthal, you need to do some washing today, so that we will have clean clothes to wear to church tonight," Berthal's mother instructed.

Berthal gathered some wood, filled the old black wash pot with water and built a fire around the pot. But her mind was a long way from washing clothes. There was a battle going on in her mind. The devil kept telling her that she did not receive the Holy Ghost. At the same time, the Lord was telling her that she did. A see-saw battle raged.

As she rubbed the clothes on the old washboard, she began to think upon God, and His goodness and began to worship Him. Suddenly soap suds flew everywhere. Berthal raised her hands and began to glorify and magnify God. She began to speak fluently in other tongues as the Spirit of God moved upon her. This forever settled in her mind her experience of the Holy Ghost. The devil could never again make her doubt the reality of the baptism of the Spirit.

"Now, Sister Berthal," Brother Goff said a few days later, "You must be baptized in Jesus' name so that your sins can be remitted. You do want to follow Jesus all the way, don't you?"

Yes, she had determined to go all the way with Him, but she was so afraid of the water. Just thinking about having water come all the way over her head made her shudder. Brother Goff realized that Berthal had a great fear of water, so he let her kneel down near the edge of the creek instead of going out in the deep water.

Brother Goff prayed over Berthal before he baptized her. She remembered his saying, "I now baptize you in the name of Jesus Christ for the remission of all of your sins."

As he lowered her backward into that water, all fear left and she felt peace as she had never felt before.

Sister Iva Mae West and Sister Mary Hill Ratchford were lady ministers who helped in some revivals that Berthal attended. They proved to be instrumental in helping shape Berthal's life. She often thought to herself, "Oh, if I could be a soul winner for Jesus like Sister West and Sister Ratchford."

On August 30, 1930, Berthal received her call to the ministry. She was nineteen years old. "Lord, I feel so unworthy," cried Berthal. "I can't even give a decent testimony."

Suddenly she heard a distinct voice out of heaven saying, "I'll go with you!"

The Lord began to give Berthal verses of Scripture to confirm her call – scriptures that she did not know were even in the Bible. There was no doubt in her mind that God had spoken to her heart concerning the ministry.

"Berthal, I would like for you to come and preach for me next Sunday," invited Brother H. L. Bennett, the pastor at Midway Pentecostal Church in Carroll County.

"Well, it'll be my first sermon, I don't know how I will do" Berthal answered, "but I'll do my best."

When Berthal sought the Lord for the service, He gave her a message which she entitled, "Some reasons why we should offer thanks unto God on thanksgiving."

"I thought I did fairly well on my first sermon," thought Berthal.

Annice, one of Berthal's sisters, had learned to pick a guitar and was quite good at the piano. Berthal convinced Annice that she should travel with her and help her evangelize by helping with the music and the singing.

Their first revival was at Poplar Corner Church in Carroll County near Lexington, Tennessee

When the services were turned over to the Jones sisters, they would sing such songs as "My, Didn't It Rain," "The Hornet Song," and "We'll Walk Through the Streets of That City." Then Berthal would preach the Word of God. Usually the altars were full of people seeking God and giving their hearts to God.

The calls for the Jones Sisters to come and preach revivals began to increase to such a point that they hardly had any time at home. They traveled far and near, especially in Tennessee, preaching and singing. Many souls were won into the kingdom of God.

One night Berthal was kneeling down on the platform illustrating how Jesus knelt at Gethsemane when the heel of her shoe got caught in her skirt, and she fell backwards. Needless to say she received a few laughs for this.

The years quickly passed for Berthal. She had been so busy working for God, being in different places preaching revivals, that she had not met anyone she would want for a husband. But God had someone for her. She had waited until she was thirty-five years old before God sent her a fine young man named Okley Crossno. Berthal and Okley were very happy. Okley proved to be a valuable asset to Berthal's ministry.

God did not see fit to send them any children, but He did make a way for them to adopt a little boy, whom they named Dale.

Dale brought even more happiness to their home than they had thought possible. As he grew into teen years, he and Okley had many happy times together. Often they would scuffle and play games of matching strength.

One night Dale wanted Berthal to scuffle with him. He was convinced that he could match his strength with hers. "Our hands were locked and we were pushing against each other," Berthal recalled, "trying to make the other one lose ground." She had not realized that her son had become so strong. When she felt herself give, she thought, "If I can get my back against the wall, I can hold my feet better."

But instead of leaning against the wall, she leaned against a door that was latched, and Berthal fell flat in the floor. How her body ached! She hobbled to bed, but she was hurting so much that she could not stay lying down. She inched her way to Dale's room, where another young man was spending the night with him, and asked them to pray for her. During that prayer, God's mercy was extended again to Berthal. She felt the pain and soreness leave, and she did not have any further trouble.

In 1944 Berthal accepted the pastorate of the First United Pentecostal Church in Camden, Tennessee. She pastored this church until 1947.

In 1957, the Lord sent her to a little country church seven miles northwest of Camden, Tennessee, called the Rushing's Chapel Pentecostal Church. They were only having one service per week when she took the church. Sister Berthal felt the need to begin a Sunday school. People began to come. The church began to grow and a revival spirit was in the air. During the year that Berthal was pastor of the Rushing's Chapel Pentecostal Church, many people came to know the Lord. There were many joyous times, and there were times of trial.

One remarkable healing in Berthal's life came while she was at Rushing's Chapel. She was having some physical problems and consulted a doctor.

"Berthal, I hate to tell you this, but you have cancer" the doctor confided. "I will schedule you for surgery."

Berthal had trusted God all these years for her needs, and she felt that it was no time now to turn from trusting Him. She said that she did not want the surgery. The doctor told her she had the fastest growing kind of cancer.

By all indications she would not have long to live. However, during the next few weeks, the mighty hand of God reached down and touched Berthal and removed the cancer.

"I can't understand it," the doctor exclaimed as he scratched his head. "I can't find any trace of cancer."

"God did it! He took care of it," Berthal assured the doctor.

"Well, it had to be God," the doctor agreed.

God certainly had his hand on Berthal, and she was faithful to work for Him. Whether it was the radio ministry, which she conducted for several years called the "Landmarks of Pentecost," or publishing a monthly paper filled with sermons or testimonies of those who had been greatly blessed of God, she was always trying to reach another lost soul.

Many times when people of the county became sick, they would call Berthal to pray for them, even though they were not Pentecostal. They knew she could touch God for them.

There was hardly a dry eye in the Rushing's Chapel Church as Berthal read her resignation as pastor after twenty-one years of labor there. Berthal was tired and the responsibility had become too great for her.

She is retired from the ministry, but her love for lost souls is still burning in her heart just as it had been since she first came in contact with Jesus Christ.

Berthal's life has touched and blessed many hundreds of people. She made the earth a better place to live. She has faithfully preached the Word of God in love and in truth while fighting the good fight of faith and keeping an eye on the crown of life that waits her when God calls her home.

Addendum:

After an extended illness, Sister Berthal Crossno passed from this life on July 20, 1998 at the LeBonheur Hospital in Jackson, Tennessee.

Her funeral was held at the First United Pentecostal Church with her pastor, Rev. Marty Johnson doing the officiating. Rev. Danny Boyd, one of the young men who was converted under her ministry spoke of the influence she had had on his life. Rev. Wayne Chester, District Superintendent of the Tennessee District was converted under her ministry, was in Washington D. C. and could not get back for the funeral but sent a letter to be read at the funeral, telling of his love and appreciation for this great saint of God.

She was laid to rest at the Pleasant Hill Cemetery located about seven miles north of Camden.

Even though Sister Berthal Crossno is gone, her influence will live on and on. The world was made a better place because of her influence on countless souls who sat under her ministry.

1942 baptismal service with C.M. Goff baptizing and W.M. Greer on right bank.

A young lady preacher (Left) Berthal Crossno Evang. In Tenn. Tent Meeting in 1940.

WILLIAM HUGH CUPPLES
June 19, 1928 – May 21, 1973
By Frances Cupples Holland

It was cotton chopping time in rural West Tennessee, just a few miles from Bemis in the Harts Bridge community. It was not any different at the Cupples farm. The land owner, W. A. Cupples, was busy keeping the farm hands working and keeping their hoes sharpened. The date was June 19, 1928. The alarm sounded signifying his wife, Lillian Sanders Cupples was in labor. She had given birth a few years earlier to a daughter, Vada Grace, so she knew the signs. With few telephones in the area, her husband left to go for the doctor. When they finally arrived back to the home they called Blue Heaven, the new big baby boy, William Hugh Cupples, had already arrived. This was not unusual in the life of William Hugh whom everyone called Bill.

Bill's childhood and adolescent years were not unlike other boys reared in the country and on the farm. There was always work to be done. At a very young age he learned how to plow the fields, drive the wagon, and then take stave bolts and farm produce into town to sell. Of course, as time progressed, there were tractors, trucks, chain saws and other farm equipment making life on the farm a little easier for everyone.

Formal education at this time consisted of grade school in the Harts Bridge community and going on to high school in Pinson.

In Bill's late teen years, the family purchased a large apple orchard and moved from Blue Heaven. The big task here was pruning, spraying the trees, and picking the fruit. The whole family worked in the business, and by this time there were three more added to their numbers, Thelma, Joe and Sandra.

Thelma was grown by this time and dating a fellow who was planning to be a Baptist minister. Howard Hutto and Robert McKeithen (known as the Hutto and McKeithen Evangelistic Party) were holding a tent revival in Henderson, Tennessee on the old shirt factory lot. Rev. J. O. Moore and his wife Doris, the daughter of our beloved Rev. A. D. Gurley, were pastoring the church in Henderson at this time. Thelma and her friend came to the revival and the Lord began to deal with her heart, and she became convicted even though she was a member of another church. She went home talking about the excitement of the service and what she felt in her heart so all the family began to attend. Her mother had been in the Pentecostal Church in Bemis during her younger years, along with her mother and dad and several other members of the family. However, she had not attended church for several years. Therefore, Bill and Thelma had not been around Pentecost and felt a real moving of the Spirit of God.

Certainly, it was not Bill's habit to attend church services. He was just a sinner boy trying to live life to it's fullest – he thought – and have a good time. Sometimes the good times turned out not being so good as was the case one weekend when he'd had a little too much fun and the police had his car. Actually, this was a blessing in disguise. He had no vehicle and none of his buddies came by to get him, so he decided to attend church with his family. The Lord began to deal with his heart and convict him of his sins. He began to go to the altar and really seek after God.

There were a lot of things in his worldly lifestyle that he struggled with and it took him a while to really dedicate and get his act together. He had a real struggle giving up his cigarettes, but after his mother went on an eleven-day fast (no food or water), God delivered him from nicotine. He never smoked another one. Thank God for praying mothers who know how to get hold of God.

The pastor, Brother Moore, continued to work with and encourage Bill. Since he had been coming to the altar and seeking God, the pastor was talking to him about water baptism in Jesus name. He had been baptized several years before in another church and felt that was good enough. Brother Moore gave him scriptures on Jesus name baptism and explained the difference in being baptized in the name of Jesus instead of the titles, but he still could not comprehend the difference nor the importance.

One Saturday afternoon when the family was away and he was at home alone, God began to move on his heart and mind. Believe me when I say picking cotton was not his favorite thing to do, but out of frustration, he got an old cotton sack and headed out to the cotton patch to be alone and think. As he picked cotton and prayed, the truth began to unfold to him, and it became very plain. The next day at church he went to Brother Moore and told him he was ready to be baptized in Jesus name. There was no baptistry in our block basement church, so on a cold, winter Sunday afternoon, a few weeks later, he was baptized in Jesus name in icy cold water. After this he really started turning his life around and dedicating more and more to God.

A few months later, there was another revival, and this was in the church. A young minister, Rex Wilcox and his wife, were the evangelists. We had a lot of young people coming, and we were asking God for a soul stirring revival. It was wintertime and everybody was busy with school, work and life in general. Twelve or fifteen people received the Holy Ghost. Bill was one of them. From this initial infilling, he spoke a very clear fluent language when he spoke in tongues. I have walked out where he was working under a car hood or on a lawn mower motor and heard him just communing with God in another language.

Immediately after being filled with the Spirit, he felt a strong calling to help other people understand how to yield themselves to receive the Holy Ghost. Well, guess who he came to first? Me, Frances Lewis, who later became his wife. I had been baptized about ten months before and still had not been filled with the Holy Spirit. He came to my house one night and talked with me. The next time I went to church, I received the infilling of the Holy Ghost. That was January 1, 1950.

Bill and I had a short courtship the summer before, but nothing serious. We had a large group of young people at that time. Yeah! You guessed it! Boy meets girl – girl meets boy, so lots of dating going on. After a little while we decided to get married. Bill's sister, Thelma, had become engaged to J. T. Plunk, so we decided to have a double wedding on May 3, 1950. We were all nervous including our pastor. This was his first wedding ceremony to perform and I still remember seeing the book he used shake in his hands. He was a very meticulous person and wanted any job he did to be done properly. I guess we had strained him somewhat by putting a double whammy on him!

Bill had talked with me some about his burden to work for God, but you know when you are in love you only hear what you want to hear. It really made me nervous when I began to realize I just might end up being a preacher's wife. Some of the girls dreamed of the day and longed to be a preacher's wife, but that was not a dream of mine. However, we had only been married a short while when he was called to preach his first sermon taken from Hebrews 12:1 ... "Let us lay aside every weight and the sin which doth so easily beset us." I don't know if he actually chose a subject, but he talked about laying aside weights that keep us from being our best in God's service. A short time later he was called on again and he used the scripture in St. John 21:15-17 where Christ asked Peter three times if he loved him, and after Peter told him yes every time, He told Peter, "If you love me, feed my sheep." I knew from that time on that his ministry would basically be pastoral.

In 1951, because no one really loved the farm and failing apple orchard business, we moved to Akron, Ohio. Bill went to work at Goodyear Aircraft.

Our first child, a darling baby girl named Ruth Ann, was born June 4, 1952. We were so thrilled and her daddy really doted over her. Regardless of all the articles we had read and all the input from those around us, neither of us had the foggiest idea of reality. I sometimes wonder how our first babies survive our "learning as we go" methods.

While in Akron, we attended a United Pentecostal Church were Rev. Delmar White was pastor. We loved the pastor and the people, but in the summer of that year, Goodyear had a shut down or a slow down and we moved back to Tennessee. Bill took an insurance job and we went back to our home church. Even though we lived in another town, we still wanted to attend and be a part of our home church.

In the meantime, the desire to preach and get more involved in full time ministry was really burning in our hearts. J. T. Plunk, Bill's brother-in-law, W. D. McCollum (J. T.'s brother-in-law), and Bill built a couple of brush arbors and held revivals. They also preached in some old store buildings and just anywhere a door was open.

A little while later a church came open and we were invited to preach and then accepted the pastorate. This was the Pentecostal Church in the Perry Switch community. Bill had to get with our Tennessee District Superintendent, Rev. W. M. Greer, to obtain a minister's license. Pastoring was a learning process for both us and the church. The Lord blessed and we had a couple revivals where several people gave their hearts to the Lord. Two of the evangelists we had were Rev. Gene White and our former Pastor, Rev. J. O. Moore.

When we got ready to baptize the converts, we used the baptistry at the Bemis Church. I don't know how nervous Bill was, but I was sure nervous. Sister Lela Holland, pastor in Lexington, had some people to baptize so she had made arrangements for Bill to baptize them for her. The females were on one side of the baptistry and the males at the other end. He baptized the females first and when the males came in, one at a time, he just baptized them the other way instead of turning them around to face the same direction the ladies had faced. I didn't think too much about it until Sister Holland's husband said to me after the service, "I thought sure he was going to baptize those men face down. I never saw anyone baptize right and left." So after that he called Bill "two-gun Pete."

The next baptismal service we had was in the Forked Deer River. It was warm and we had a large crowd on Sunday afternoon. Bill was baptizing several in one family and when he put the father under, he was wearing a long sleeved shirt, and Bill saw the dry sleeve, so he just dunked him under again.

We had moved out in the country by some of the church people, the David Dorris family and Horace Simmons family. The day before (Sunday) Bill had been sick and had the church deacons anoint him with oil and pray for him. The spirit of God moved and David Dorris was shouting and jumping. The next day I looked out in the sand pile where Ruth Ann and David's son Ronnie were playing, and Ronnie had his hands on Ruth Ann's head and was jumping just like he'd see the day before at church. It was comical in a way, but I had a feeling if she had really been sick, she very likely would have been healed. You could see and feel the sincerity. We stayed at Perry Switch about a year and some of those people are still my dear friends.

One Sunday morning we were on our way to church and stopped for gas. Bill came back to the car and told me Brother Douglas had a heart attack and was in bad shape. He was pastoring the church at Trenton, Tennessee. We had been having a lean time financially, and Bill was to start a new insurance job in Brownsville the next morning. There was no UPC Church there and he and Brother Greer had discussed the possibility of starting a church there. Bill had told me on Sunday that he'd have to go to Trenton and help out there and eventually pastor. It sure looked doubtful and I told him that he would sure be stepping into some mighty big shoes, following Brother Kenneth Reeves and Brother E. J. Douglas. Imagine when he went into the insurance office the next morning to start his new job and the manager asked him if he would consider going somewhere besides Brownsville! He said, "we've had some changes take place, and we'd like to have you in Trenton." Imagine our feelings if you can! Within two weeks, we had rented an apartment and moved to Trenton and started attending the church there. Bill preached quite a bit for Brother Douglas and when he resigned Bill was elected pastor. He worked at being a successful pastor. He spent a lot of time studying, praying and getting to know the people. There were problems he had to work with and try to iron out, but we had a move of God and God blessed our efforts. We had great fellowship in the area and harmony in the church.

God had begun to deal with Bill's heart about going to Africa as a missionary some years prior, but we both realized we would need experience and some seasoning before we would be ready for that kind of endeavor. When Bill went to the next General Conference, he met the Missionary Board and presented his burden. They advised him to attend Bible College. He called a church meeting and presented his burden to them and they agreed for us to attend Bible College and continue pastoring. So, he enrolled in Pentecostal Bible Institute in Tupelo, Mississippi. For several months we were at school through the week and back home on weekends. We really appreciated the church's kindness but felt we were doing them a disservice so we resigned.

In May of that year we took a couple of days off from school and went to St. Louis to meet the missionary board again. This was his third meeting and my first. Several church leaders and older ministers told us that we were too young and inexperienced and would not be approved. But again, it was God's timing and we were approved to go to Liberia, West Africa. At the meeting, Bill was asked if he thought he could learn to fly an airplane. His answer was, "Yes, I can drive a truck and a tractor, and I believe I can learn to fly an airplane."

As soon as school was out, we moved to Bemis. Flight training was begun at McKellar Field. Bill loved it but also knew and respected the danger involved.

This first airplane ever purchased by the United Pentecostal Church, a Piper Tri Pacer, was chosen because of its ability to do short landings and take offs. The manufacturers flew it to Jackson, so Bill could acquaint himself with the same plane he would be flying in Liberia.

We traveled the next several months visiting churches and trying to express our burden to others. Most of our visiting was in Tennessee, and most of our financial support for our first term was from the Tennessee District. They also purchased most of our equipment that we would need.

We left in December on board the ship, the Del Rio, with Sister Georgia Regenhardt. She was a veteran missionary who had traveled with us some and had been a real blessing in helping us prepare for the field. We were seventeen days enroute which included Christmas. After arriving at the Freeport of Liberia at Monrovia, we had to spend two nights anchored outside the breakwaters before we could disembark because there were many ships ahead of us. It was a glad day when we finally got to set foot on the ground again. We were met at the port by Brother Jack Langham, Sister Valda Russell, and Sister Geneva Bailey. I know now but didn't realize then, they were really watching us to see how we responded to the culture shock. And believe me, it was shocking.

Our first home was in Bomi Hill at the mission station there. Brother and Sister Langham and their children and Sister Russell were the resident missionaries. The house that Brother Langham and the nationals had built was far beyond our expectations. We had cement floors and metal roof which was a sign of affluence and also a cement bathtub.

We realized that being able to work with other missionaries and learn from them was a real value to us. We tried to fit into the work and learn what we needed to do to further the work of Christ and reach the lost. The mission station maintained a school, a church, a boarding place for students and a village outreach.

After several months at Bomi Hill we obtained permission to move interior and build a work in an unevangelized area. The name of the village was Bella Yella (pronounced belly). There was a branch of the Liberian Military and a prison there also.

We lived in the village and really roughed it – I mean – REALLY. Bill went in with some of the gospel workers from the Fassama Mission Station about a month before Ruth Ann and I ever moved. He was trying to make the house a little more commodious for us. It was the only house in the village with a metal roof. It shed the water but also was much warmer than the regular thatch roofs. Liberia has six months rain time and six months dry weather. The metal roof was definitely valuable in rain time.

We were having services three or four times a week in the largest pavilion in the village. The people were attending well and God was blessing our efforts. The work was just getting off to a good start, when we were visited by our Missions Director, Rev. Wynn T. Stairs. He felt we should move on over the mountain to Fassama, because it was almost furlough time for Sister Gruse, and he did not want to have a lone, single lady at that station again. A few years before Sister Pauline Gruse and Sister Laverne Collins were there, and Sister Collins got sick and passed away before Sister Gruse could get word to our other missionaries, so she had to prepare the body and bury her with just the help of the nationals.

We moved on over the mountain, a ten-minute flight and a day's walk. Thankfully, we never had to walk it, but Sister Gruse and Sister Bailey walked it several times. Our hats were "off" to those two ladies. They had gone into the depths of this hinterland and not only raised up a soul saving station, but with the help of the nationals, built a very lovely mission station.

It took us a few months to get a house built, and in the meantime we lived in a two-room mud house with dirt floors and a separate little hut for our kitchen. We had gotten our kerosene refrigerator in and could now have ice cold water and tea. We could have given up almost anything in our house more easily than the fridge.

While we were living there, I was on the little screened in porch teaching Ruth Ann, and one of the schoolgirls came up and was really surprised that the white girl had to be schooled. The national language was English, and she thought because Ruth Ann knew English that she also knew "the book", as they called getting an education.

Pretty soon it became evident that the missionaries were expecting an addition to the family. Of course, we were thrilled, but it seemed that all of the mission station was excited. After lots of ups and downs, which is another time-consuming story, William Edward Cupples was added to our family on January 7, 1959. I went down to the Bomi Hill station to be near the hospital and when I finally got back to Fassama with him, everybody in the village and the mission was really eager to see him. He was the first white baby that most of them had ever seen.

When Eddie was six months old, because of my need for surgery, we came back to the states on furlough. When we finally got back to Tennessee, it was almost camp meeting time. It was heavenly to be back home and in camp meeting again.

After the surgery, we traveled in order to give our work publicity among our churches and raise our support for our next term of service. During the school year, Bill mostly traveled alone and I stayed home in Henderson to keep Ruth Ann in school.

We were home one and one-half years and then returned to Liberia via the Del Sol. This was really a rough voyage and because of the turbulence, we were unable to even be on the deck very much. That little room got smaller every day, so again we were really glad to disembark and get our feet on solid ground.

Since we had our house ready, the main project was to assemble the new plane that had been purchased and get it air ready. The first plane had been wrecked after we left. Brother Langham, Bill and one of his friends, a missionary pilot with the Assemblies of God, Brother Crabough, assembled the plane. Their mission station was on the motor road as it was called. So after they got it air ready, they took it out on the road and had some of the guys to stop traffic at both ends and flew the plane right off the road. This was a very daring thing to do but sometimes your choices were limited. After a few hours in the air, Bill and Brother Langham flew a trip into Fassama. Then in a day or so we went in as a family to start our second term. Sister Gruse was back on the field and had our house ship-shape. No, not like here, but you learn to live and make do wherever you are planted. Bill was several days in getting our supplies and equipment into the station. We had taken in a diesel generator, a gasoline pump to put in the creek and pump water to our station, all the plastic pipe for the system plus other things to make life a little easier and more pleasant.

The Langhams had lost their daughter, Sharon, in a tragic accident while we were on furlough. We all felt the loss very keenly when we returned, but Ruth Ann really missed her. Sister Langham and I were very close. She wanted to fly into Fassama and stay a week and help me. She was a real blessing helping me get unpacked and straightened up. She said she really needed the time away and an opportunity to talk her heart out.

We spent Christmas time at the Langham's along with Sister Russell and Sister Gruse. We tried to maintain as much American tradition as possible. The fellows liked to get a lot of fireworks, and you could really get some pretty ones and powerful ones. This was kind of the highlight of the holiday fun.

After Christmas, it was back to Fassama and reentering the work there. We saw hard times and good times in the next five years. One of the hardest things we did was to send Ruth Ann home. We had hoped for replacements in six months, but things did not work out as planned and it was a year and a half before we saw her again.

There were many times we had a refreshing from God. There were two real miracles that I want to relate. One morning we were having a terrible tropical storm. It was thundering and lightening almost constantly. We had to close the shutters and windows and light the lanterns to even be able to see how to cook breakfast. There was a terrible cracking sound, and we knew the lightening had struck somewhere really close. In just a minute, some of the mission boys came hollering, "Brother Cupples, Brother Cupples – Mother Gruse, Mother Gruse." Bill took off running behind the two boys as fast as he could and as soon as I could reassure Ruth Ann and Eddie, I took off behind him. On the screened in veranda of her house, Sister Gruse lay on the floor – her face shriveled and contorted, her body drawn, her knees drawn up on either side of her neck. She looked terrible! Bill was on his knees beside her, and he looked up at me and said, "Honey, she's dead." I went totally numb. He said to me and all the mission family gathered around, "Pray, pray, pray." Like I said, we were all numb, and all we could say was "Jesus, Jesus, Jesus." Bill was still kneeling beside her calling on the Lord. This lasted several minutes and seemed like eternity. She began to open her eyes. Her arms and legs began to gradually straighten out, and like a slow motion movie, her face began to take normal shape again. We were all saying. "Thank you Jesus, hallelujah, Praise God!"

Her testimony, also given in her book *I Surrender All* (pp. 292-295 by Pauline Gruse), reinforced the fact that she literally was dead. She said she felt life leave her body and that she was basking in the glory and presence of God. The peace she felt was unparalleled to anything she had felt before. She could feel herself suspended somewhere between heaven and earth. She looked down and could see her body lying there on the floor. She told the Lord she was coming home, and he spoke to her and told her that he was not through with her. Bill helped her raise to a sitting position when she told everyone standing that she had been dead, but God brought her back to life. She lived until 1998.

Another miracle was the opening of Tiddybaugh's blinded eyes, a national child that had gotten some carbide in the metal container, put some water in it, and put in the open fire. It exploded burning him severely on his face and eyes. He could not see. They brought him to the mission several days later for him to be flown to the hospital. He was on his mother's back and they lifted the cloth for us to see him. I had to leave because of the sight and I was crying so much. We got to the plane hangar. Bill stopped all the onlookers and believers and had prayer for Tiddybaugh asking God to intervene and do a miracle. He took him on to the hospital and the missionary doctor took one look at him and after checking him said, "I can treat the burned flesh, but it will take months for healing, and he will never see again." Bill had to go back in a couple of weeks, and Tiddybaugh was sitting up in his bed. The doctor said to come and see the miracle that had taken place. The boy can see and the burns are healing remarkably. In a few weeks he was back home and brought thank you gifts to the missionary. Our last account of him, he was preaching the gospel.

Sister Else Lund had come to work with us at Fassama and was so willing to do whatever was necessary. She taught our school and ministered as well. Ruth Ann and Eddie loved her dearly. She also helped Ruth Ann with some of her schooling.

When it was furlough time we knew we would not be returning. Brother Oscar Vouga, the missions director, had asked us to consider Jamaica or Hawaii. He needed someone both places. But God had other plans for our lives. Bill told me one day in the workshop that we would be coming home to pastor at our home church in Henderson. I had learned by this time that when he told me God had spoken and given him direction that I could believe it and just wait for it to happen.

Well, within six months he had been elected pastor and we had moved into the parsonage. It was not smooth sailing at first, but after awhile we began to have revival and it was with a heavy heart that we were to leave.

One morning after passing through Savannah the preceding night, we received a phone call. The voice on the other end was from Savannah. Rev. W. H. Deberry asked if we would consider coming to Savannah. Bill told him we were perfectly happy in Henderson and had not thought about moving, but that he would pray about it. We received yet another call and Bill started to tell him "No," but he felt a sudden check in the spirit and told them he would consider it. Well, within a few weeks we had accepted the pastorate and moved to Savannah.

Bill's ministry and methods were unique in many ways. The people soon learned that he was interested in their souls and welfare in general. Pastoring was never a "job" with him, it was a calling seasoned with a burden and a deep love. God blessed our ministry here. Some 25 to 35 people had come into the church, among them several young couples.

Bill began to raise our monthly missionary pledge periodically, and I could see what was in the making. Pretty soon we were in St. Louis again appearing before the missionary board. Ruth Ann had attended the Bible College in Florissant, Missouri for a year and when we went to pick her up from school, the board was in session. Sister Gruse was there phasing our her last term and wanted us to appear with her before the board. Bill told them of his desire and calling to go to Kenya, East Africa and plans were made for us to meet with them the next session. We were approved and appointed. We resigned the Savannah church in December 1971 and started our deputation in January 1972. During the time at Savannah, the Tennessee District organized the Foreign Missions Department and asked Bill to serve as the first Foreign Missions Director. He accepted, but only served one year before returning to Africa. On October 19th, we (Bill, Eddie and I) boarded Pan Am in Memphis, Tennessee bound for Kenya via Liberia.

Ruth Ann had married the month before, a very fine Christian young man, Billy W. Gant, fondly called "Butch." He has been a Godsend to us.

We went to Liberia and spent a week with the missionaries there. It was good seeing everyone again and rejoicing that we could see fruits of our labors there. Now it was on to Nairobi, Kenya for a five-year tenure we thought. However, somehow in God's divine plan this was not to be.

We were met at the airport by Rev. John H. Harris and wife, Jerrie, at midnight. They had been able to rent an apartment for us right across the street from them. Brother Harris and Bill had an immediate love and respect for one another. The Harrises had formerly served in Ethiopia but when the missionaries all had to leave, they were placed in Kenya to serve with us.

Living conditions were much better living in the city instead of the hinterland. We appreciated all the comforts. Brother Harris and Bill were busy almost everyday trying to purchase or acquire some property for our church and Bible College. There was a lot of red tape to all of it, but they finally found property that could be purchased. In the meantime, we were having services in a rented YMCA room and could only hold service for a limited time. We were all frustrated with this, but had to work according to the rules.

Sheaves for Christ had purchased a Pugeot 504 automobile for us. So now Brother Harris did not have to make two trips to get us to church. Because of rigid government rules, no one was allowed to have meetings after dark without being approved. You had to acquire a permit and be licensed with the government. All of this takes time. Bill's "preacher's itch" was really bothering him. He and Brother Harris were able to get permits to one of the largest housing complexes in the city. They would preach and we'd sing, Bill with his guitar and Jerrie with her accordion. We were allowed to use a public address system and were having 400 to 500 people in these Sunday afternoon services. Bill's last sermon was preached here and his topic was "When God Calls."

The fellows were preaching and teaching in Nairobi but also went to Western Kenya to visit churches there. They taught Jesus name baptism and after another trip, baptized 16 trinity preachers in Jesus name. They wanted to bring their groups in and affiliate with the UPC.

On May 21, 1973, our Africa Director, Rev. E. L. Freeman and his wife, Nona were picked up at the airport by Brother Harris and Bill. They came to our house after flying all night from the Camaroons. We had breakfast and they lay down and slept awhile. The fellows had scheduled services in Western Kenya to preach and teach in the new churches there.

The Harrises came over. We all had lunch and the fellows got ready to leave. We all stood in our living room, held hands and prayed. I distinctly remember hearing Bill ask God to "grant them traveling mercies" as they traveled. The men kissed their wives goodbye, got in the car, and as they pulled out of the driveway, he slapped the side of the car and told Eddie to get on those books. Little did we realize that would be his last words to us.

A few hours down the road, he was killed in a tragic accident. He left a legacy that is priceless as far as his family is concerned. He preached what he believed and lived by what he preached. The late Rev. Oscar Vouga spoke it this way – "He was a prince of a man and a genuine Christian."

There is a church and Bible college in Nairobi dedicated to his memory.

154 Tennessee District Heritage

The Cupples Family: Eddie, Frances, Bill and Ruth Ann.

Bro. & Sis. Cupples at the Perryville Camp Ground in 1972

Bro. Cupples and Bro. McCollum, 1959.

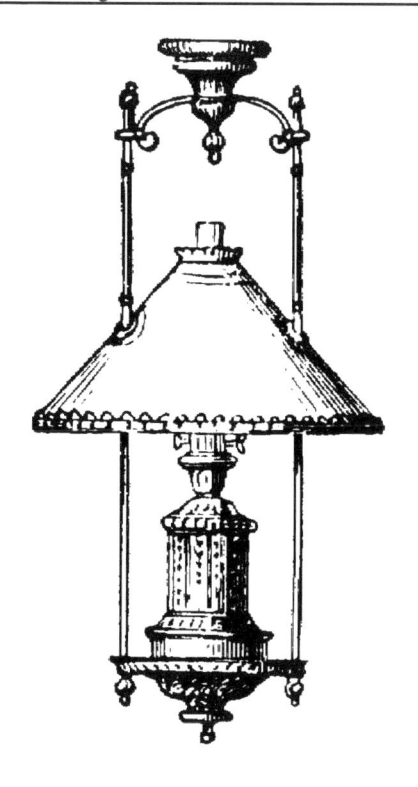

Biographies of Deceased Department Leaders and some of the early Presbyters

ROY G. BOLING
By Pearl Boling

Roy Boling was born July 25, 1917 to Cord and Annie Ross Boling in Sardis, Tennessee. His mother died of typhoid fever when he was four years old. After her death, Roy, his younger sister, and their father lived in his grandfather's home.

In November 1935, Roy married Dorothy Harwell. Two years later in November 1937, their only child, a son was born. They chose the name of Neal for this special boy.

Brother Boling grew up attending the Methodist Church in Morris Chapel with his grandparents. He was introduced to Pentecost when Dorothy's brother, James Harwell, took Roy to church where Brother Cleo Kelly was holding a revival at Vernon's Chapel, south of Lexington, Tennessee. Brother and Sister Boling repented in a revival at Scott's Hill in 1936. He received the Holy Ghost and soon after acknowledged his call to preach. He had been rejected by the military draft board because of bad health. But the Lord took the "Military Reject" and made a Godly, dedicated, soul-winning preacher of him! When he told Brother Kelly about his call to the ministry, Brother Kelly replied that he already knew it. Brother Kelly assisted him in beginning his ministry by arranging a one-week revival in a new church he had started.

For several years, Brother Boling and Brother B. L. Hollin held revivals in brush arbors, store fronts, school houses, and on front porches. After a second tent revival at Milledgeville, where approximately forty converts were baptized in the Tennessee River at Saltillo, they asked him to be their pastor. From that time, his ministry was devoted mostly to pastoral work. He became a part of the Pentecostal Church, Inc. in 1940. When Tennessee became a District, he served on the District Board for about three years.

After he pastored at Milledgeville, he pastored several churches in the area including Adamsville, Mt. Carmel, Mt. Tabor, Enville, Morris Chapel, Beacon, Natchez Trace and Beauty Hill.

In 1956, he became caretaker of the Pentecostal Camp Ground at Perryville, Tennessee. He not only took care of the existing buildings but helped to build a new dining hall, a Ladies Lounge, and repaired and remodeled several buildings. His experience as a carpenter helped very much in the growth of the Campground.

His wife of 45 years passed away in 1980. In 1981, he married Pearl Groves of Memphis, Tennessee. With her dedication and help, his ministry continued to be a blessing. They began a church at Natchez Trace in 1984. He actually built the church building while they lived in a motor home near the site. He pastored this church until 1986 and Brother O. L. Hicks became their pastor after Brother Boling resigned.

Brother Boling was elected pastor again at Beauty Hill in 1986 and pastored until 1989. Many miracles of the saving power of God were witnessed during his ministry.

There was no complete record of baptisms and healings that happened as results of his preaching and faith. Only heaven's records will reveal his accomplishments.

In his last years he was severely crippled with arthritis and was unable to do much preaching. He and Sister Pearl made their home in Adamsville and attended church services as often as his health allowed. Brother Boling died on May 8, 1999 at the age of 81. His funeral was held at the Crump Pentecostal Church. He had fulfilled his calling with 55 years as a faithful minister of the Gospel of his Lord and Saviour, Jesus Christ. His life exemplified his personal motto: *Only one life twill soon be past, Only what's done for Christ will last!*

Roy Boling, Perryville Camp Caretaker.

Rev. & Mrs. Vannie Spencer, Sis. Pearl and Bro. Roy Boling.

Bro. & Sis. Roy Boling standing before the church they built at Natchez Trace in 1984.

GEORGE L. GLASS
By Myrtise Glass

In the small town of Robeline, Louisiana on July 17, 1909, a male child was born to R. H. (Bob) Glass and Daisy Vascoquo Glass. They named him George Lafayette. He and his older sister, Blanche, were left without a mother when he was only two or three years old. She died at the birth of their third child; the baby also died. George and Blanche soon knew the love of a mother once again. Bob married Allie Richey, who was never referred to as a stepmother. Brother Glass always said he was placed in the arms of an angel. The family grew to include other brothers and sisters: Gladys, Bill, Arless, Lucille, Medford and Charles.

Little did Bob and Allie realize the impact their oldest son would have on the work of God, not only in the state of Louisiana but also around the world. For in the year 1933, in the month of January, George L. Glass began a ministry that has grown and enlarged until the demands of that ministry caused him to become acquainted with and drawn into every facet of the work and outreach of the United Pentecostal Church.

At the tender age of 23, he was active in evangelistic ministry in DeRidder and neighboring communities. This was still "early days" in our Pentecostal history, and we had very few churches. We were yet in the depression era, and few people owned automobiles. If you had a job, you were very fortunate. The young preacher was blessed to be working in a hardwood-flooring factory. When the five o'clock whistle blew, he would rush home, bathe, dress, grab a bite to eat, and get out on the road to thumb a ride with a local merchant who would be driving out to his country home. Brother Glass would flag him down and ask, "May I ride as far as Brother Slaydon's house? I'm preaching there tonight on his front porch. We would love to have you there."

The merchant always replied, "I guess you can ride that far." There was no friendliness from this man toward his passenger, but the evangelist could not afford to allow this to affect him. He kept up a cheerful banter until Brother Slaydon's house came into view, and he would say, "Well, here we are." The old man would stop to let him out, shift gears, and drive away without a word. He did attend the services though. He would stand back on the edge of the crowd in the shadows to grumble, heckle, and always say, "You won't have a preacher tomorrow night; he rides out with me, and I'm not going to bring him out here to preach that rotten doctrine!"

This didn't seem to bother the young preacher. After spending the night with the Slaydon family, he would be out on the road the next morning when the merchant came driving along, thumbing a ride back into town, to home, and on to the plant.

Many hot afternoons found young Brother Glass hiking along the highway to get to his next preaching service. Blistered feet caused him to stop many times along the road to take off his shoes and continue walking. No car came along to pick him up. When he would get within view of his preaching place, he would stop, dust off his feet, put on his socks and shoes, don his coat, and arrive ready to preach.

The offerings received for him were *large.* As much as 100, 200 and even 300 pennies would weigh his pockets down, to the extent it was hard not to have "holey pockets."

Summer preaching was a breeze! It was cooler on the porches. In the winter they would move into the front or fireplace room. The preacher was always placed in front of the fireplace. The roaring fire kept him well roasted on the backside. A love for souls made all these inconveniences of no consequence. There are many Pentecostal churches in that area today, and many people will never know the great price paid to bring them into existence.

In the first year of his evangelistic ministry, Brother Glass accepted his first pastorate -- a little church near DeRidder at Bethel Grove. This proved to be a turning point and a landmark in many people's lives. He continued to work in the flooring plant.

When Brother Glass received the Holy Ghost, persecution of the "holy rollers" was the order of the day, and he did not escape this rule. When he arrived at work to start his machine at 8:00 a.m., it was not to be shut down until the lunch hour. The men at the machines on either side, in front or behind you, would watch his neighbor's machine for him to take a restroom break. Not so for Brother Glass! If he so much as looked up, all the men around would clap their hands at him, or raise their hands in mockery of praise to taunt him. What they did not know was the fact that God was using all this. Brother Glass's supervisor was observing him very closely.

One day someone came up behind him. Strong hands grasped his arms, pinning them to his sides. Above the roar of the machinery, a voice in his ear was saying. "The folk out at the church are in for a surprise tonight!" Brother Glass first thought was, "Oh, is he going to disturb and try to ruin the meeting?" By this time his captor had released his hold enough that Brother Glass could turn, and he looked into the eyes of his employer. There were tears in his supervisor's eyes, and he heard him say, "I'm going to the altar tonight." Then he turned and moved on in his duties.

Needless to say, the young evangelist did not lose any time getting to service that night. Sure enough, his employer, George O. Dion, a business man well known in the area for his strength of character, was in church. He came to the altar and received the Holy Ghost. He came to be not only a pillar in the church, but a tower of strength and support to Brother Glass's ministry. It was nothing for Brother Dion to go up to Brother Glass's machine, turn it off, hand his car keys to him and say, "You have done enough here today; now go visit and work in the interest of the church." It was something to see the look on the face of his persecutors who would not relieve him for a restroom break. Brother Dion's brother, Crylle, became one of our ministers and pastors.

The year 1934 brought another change in his life when he accepted the pastorate in Many, Louisiana. In 1936, he moved on to Faith Tabernacle in Port Arthur, Texas.

During his years of pastoring, he served his church organization in various capacities. In 1936, he was elected secretary-treasurer to the South Central District of Pentecostal Churches, Incorporated and was elected District Superintendent in 1938. He served while continuing to pastor the Port Arthur Church. He resigned the superintendency in 1940 but was re-elected to serve the organization as secretary-treasurer. After the merger into The United Pentecostal Church, he became secretary-treasurer of the Louisiana District. He served a total of 22 years in this office.

In 1945, Brother Glass was called to pastor his home church in DeRidder, Louisiana. Surely the Spirit led him to pray, "Oh, God, let the effect of this church be felt around the world." Soon the missionary offerings moved from dollars to hundreds until the church was giving thousands into the missionary outreach. The record says that God had his way in that prayer of the Spirit.

Also in 1945, he was appointed to serve as Associate Foreign Missionary Director of The United Pentecostal Churches, International. Many missionaries were sent to the field of their calling. Much money had to be raised, and God used Brother Glass in this endeavor. Several trips were made to British West Indies and Alaska (before Alaska was a state) in the interest of foreign missions. Along with all this, many late hours were spent with the elders of our organization in compilation of the Manual and By-laws which our organization still functions by today.

It was with a heavy heart that Brother Glass resigned his home church in 1953 to answer a call to the First Pentecostal Church of Baton Rouge, Louisiana. During all his pastorates, he carried on an active radio ministry.

After 11 years on the Foreign Missionary Board, he relinquished the position in 1956 when elected to serve as National Home Missions Director for the United States and Canada. This was a very busy time.

On October 21, 1958, in Indianapolis, Indiana, Brother Glass and Myrtise Fleming Watkins were married. Rev. E. W. Caughron performed the wedding ceremony. Sister

Glass became a great helpmeet not only in his ministry but also in her own ministry as a teacher, secretary and writer.

The Home Missions ministry carried him through all states, six Canadian Provinces, and Alaska. He came to be known for his "Home Missionary Rallies." This was before the days of jet travel. It took more than an overnight trip to get to a field.

On a trip from Baton Rouge to Alaska, via Seattle, to Juneau, to Sitka, he arrived with all luggage lost. He had no Bible or change of clothes and was to speak within ten minutes at Sitka University. He was embarrassed when the missionaries received an offering to buy him a change of clothing. In the university services a certain young lady was among those receiving the Holy Ghost. She married a man who became the Alaskan District Superintendent. Another highlight of this trip was being marooned aboard our missionary vessel, "The Madura," riding out a storm on the waters of Chatam Strait off the Alaskan Coast, and finally being flown out.

In the fifties Tupelo Children's mansion came into being. Brother Glass was an active participant in this endeavor and served on the Mansion Board of Directors.

In 1958, Brother Glass resigned the Home Missions Directorship in order to accept the pastorate of the United Pentecostal Church in Jonesboro, Arkansas. From there he was called to the Bemis Pentecostal Church in Jackson, Tennessee in 1962. This was the third church where he followed pastors who went full time to District Superintendency. While at the Bemis Church, he was appointed Home Missions Director of the Tennessee District.

It was also during this time of living and pastoring in Tennessee that his friend of many years, Elder A. D. Varnado, encouraged him to again visit Jamaica to help strengthen the churches there. This he did in 1967 and the Jamaican people were greatly blessed of the Lord through his ministry.

He resigned the Bemis Church, his largest congregation to that date, in 1968 at the age of 58 and entered the evangelistic field. He was actively engaged in this work for three years. These years are considered the most fruitful for souls of any years in his ministry. He left this field to answer another call to his home church in DeRidder to again go through an extensive building program. During all the building with various churches, many souls were born into the Kingdom of God. Over and over, consecration to serve was made. Serving the people of these churches required much study which has been passed to others through a mighty teaching ministry.

Some of the ministers who came into Pentecost under his ministry are Brothers T. F. Tenney; his sons, George L. and James R. Glass; his brothers, Arless and Charles Glass; C. E. Cooley; Benford Burnett; Edward Goins; Joe Johnson; Rufus (Scooter) Simmons; Robert Lacey; Crylle Dion and others.

February of 1972 found the Glass's in Tokyo, Japan, the Philippine Islands and Hawaii. Brother T. F. Tenney, Foreign Missions Director, honored Brother Glass by asking him to be the speaker for the first Southwestern Pacific and Asian Regional Missionary Conference.

God led Brother Glass to resign the DeRidder Church in 1976. He was elected Pastor Emeritus for life.

In December 1979 through January 1980, he was very active for the Missionary Department in New Zealand and Australia where he spoke 32 times in 32 days. Sister Glass accompanied him on these trips, and she spoke 30 times in those 32 days.

In 1975, Brother Glass was honored to be the devotional speaker on the annual School of Missions staff which allows a personal acquaintance with our missionaries.

While still sharing in the work at the DeRidder Church, there were periods of teaching at Texas Bible College, the Puerto Rican and St. Croix Churches, district seminars, interim pastorship, camp meetings and speaking in special services, etc. Brother and Sister Glass ministered in conferences in San Jose, Costa Rico in August 1982.

Time does not permit an "in-depth" story of this man's full and rewarding life, however, a short summary on the history of Rev. George L. Glass, Sr. reads as follows: From January of 1933 until May 26, 1982 in the 50th year of his ministry, he served as Evangelist, Pastor, District Superintendent, District Secretary-Treasurer, Associate Foreign Missionary Director, National Home Missions Director, on the board of Tupelo Children's Mansion, Camp Meeting Speaker (having preached in 75 to 100 camp meetings), District Home Missions Director, had a radio ministry, attended 45 of our International Conferences where he served on various committees, devotional speaker at Annual School of Missions, instructor at Texas Bible College and served our Missionary Department on various fields.

Brother Glass departed this life on Saturday evening, March 17, 1990. His life has proven that the true calling of a Christian is not to do extra-ordinary things, but to do ordinary things in an extra ordinary way or manner. His is one life of many in our ranks which has proven that God has always had a "Man with a Mission."

George Glass spoke sternly to the young man on the camp ground: "Son, if you care anything about that girl you learn to open car doors for her and attend to her like you do care for her!"

What he spoke was what he practiced. You seldom ever saw Bro. or Sis. Glass apart from each other. And Bro. Glass was always attentive to her in the special way only a gentleman could be.

A. N. GRAVES

Written and submitted by Bethel Graves Cox, great-niece of A.N. Graves, who was greatly assisted in the research for the article by her parents, A. D. Graves, Jr. and Eleanor Jean Graves.

Alvis Newt Graves was born on March 18, 1893, in Perry County, Tennessee, and moved with his family to Eaton, Gibson County, Tennessee, (near Trenton) about 1900. His parents were George Brown Graves and Martha Caroline Whitwell Graves. He was the eighth born of their children and two sisters were later added to the family to total four sons and six daughters. J.B., the first born, and Delpha E., the tenth born child, each died at two weeks old. Therefore, Newt grew up with Ida, born November 8, 1879; William Pitts, born October 22, 1881; Mattie, born September 21, 1883; Eliza A., born September 24, 1886; Minnie Lee, born September 6, 1888; Addison Dickson, known as "Bud", born August 25, 1890; and a sister named Jimmie E., born September 18, 1895.

Newt grew up on the farm. His father was a farmer and his parents were church-going people of the Baptist persuasion. They taught their children by example and wanted the best for them.

When Newt was a very small boy, probably four or five years old, he had a conflict with his brother, Bud, who was just two and a half years older than he was. They were playing on the front porch of their house at the time. Newt exclaimed, "Cuss, cuss, cuss! I guess I've cussed you, now!" His mother quickly stepped forward, grasped him by the arm and pulled him out into the front yard, where she soundly spanked him. Someone in the family said, "He wasn't actually cursing." Mother Graves responded, "Well, he thought he was cursing." She spanked him for the intent of his heart and attempted to train him to control his tongue and his temper.

Despite the diligent training given through the formative years, Newt continued to make decisions that disappointed his family. As an adult he began to frequent the "poolroom" at Trenton. The establishment was owned by Tack Nail and was frequented by persons of poor reputation. The bootlegger was usually to be found there, making his goods available to whomever wished to purchase liquor. Newt's father, mother and all his siblings were mortified that Newt spent time at the poolroom.

One evening in May 1915, after spending time at the poolroom, Newt suggested to his rowdy young friends that they go to see the show at the local theatre. When they exited the theatre, Newt said to his friends, "Now let's go see this other show!" He was speaking of the tent revival being conducted in Trenton by Rev. E.J. Douglas and Rev. W.M. Mills. They were just curious to see what was going on there, having heard that people were acting strangely, and perhaps were thinking of creating a disturbance. They walked over to the tent and stood on the outside of the tent to observe the preaching and worship that was in progress. Newt was slain by the power of God and fell to the ground. He awoke to a realization that his life must change.

And change it did, he became hungry for the Holy Ghost and began to seek the infilling of the Holy Ghost with the evidence of speaking in tongues. Fifty years later, Newt wrote a short account of his experience and titled it: *The Greatest Event of My Life*. I will quote from it throughout the remainder of the narrative, being careful to show Rev. Graves' words in italics.

THE GREATEST EVENT OF MY LIFE
By Rev. A. N. Graves

The year of 1915 the month of May, Rev. E.J. Douglas and Rev. W.M. Mills came to Trenton, Tennessee, and pitched a gospel tent. They began to preach a life free from sin and that people could receive the Holy Ghost Baptism and speak with other tongues like they did at Pentecost. This was something we had never heard before. We had been taught that it was only for the early church. The people of other churches became stirred about it and some began to speak against it. Many false rumors were created about this meeting and what was going on. Out of curiosity I went out to see if the things I had heard were really true. To my surprise I found things to be entirely different to what I had heard. They were the happiest people I had ever seen. Their faces really shined with the glory of God. I found that they were preaching the Bible and giving chapters and verses for what they taught. Pretty soon I became convinced that they had the truth. I became hungry for the experience of the Holy Ghost Baptism. I began to seek for this experience. I also heard for one to receive such an experience, that one must thoroughly repent of his sins and take up his cross and follow the Lord daily. This I did and the Lord gloriously filled me with the Holy Ghost.

Newt's old friends were amazed at the startling change in his life. One day they were at the poolroom bemoaning the fact to Tack Nail that they had lost Newt to the Pentecostals. Mr. Nail said, "Don't worry, boys. Newt will be back. Newt will be back." Newt never went back to the boys at the poolroom; he had joined the gospel band of believers and had found a new life in Jesus Christ.

He was called into the ministry and began to preach the gospel immediately after receiving the Holy Ghost. At the time of his conversion, Newt was employed by Professor

Dennison, an educated man, who owned a dairy in Trenton. Newt sold the dairy products: milk, butter, cheese, etc. for him. He sold these items from a horse and cart or sometimes sold them from a wheelbarrow. He filled the wheelbarrow with the dairy products and pushed the wheelbarrow from house to house on his route. People in the community said that Professor Dennison was an atheist. After Newt's conversion, his employer said, "I'm thoroughly convinced that a man must be called of God to preach. Newt is a called preacher." Professor Dennison recognized that God had changed Newt completely and had enabled a man without much formal education to become an anointed, powerful preacher!

Newt's transformation was noticed immediately by his family. The wife of Newt's brother, Bud, Beulah Walker Graves, said that they were glad that Newt was giving up his life of sin, but that they were shocked that he had taken up with the Pentecostals. All of the Graves were Baptist and were ashamed that many of the preachers that Newt was connected with were very poor. Beulah said that she would become so angry when she heard Newt calling them "brother" and "sister". She said that she thought he should find people of a higher class with whom to associate.

One summer night in 1915, Bud hitched the horse and buggy and took his mother to Memphis, Tennessee, to visit his brother, Pitts and his wife, Bernice. While they were gone to Memphis, Beulah stayed with Bud's sister, Minnie and her husband, Sam Graves. Brother E. J. Douglas was holding a tent revival at Edison, Tennessee, which is near Trenton and very near Sam and Minnie's house. They went out to the revival with Newt. While the service was in progress and Beulah was seated inside the tent, she said that the Spirit of the Lord fell on her and she began to worship the Lord with all her heart and to dance before the Lord.

She said that the most unusual sound that she had ever heard began to come forth from her throat and mouth, she said that she could only compare it to a turkey gobbling. When she came to herself, she had danced outside the tent into the cornfield and Newt was on his knees in front of her. She asked, "Newt, what in the world has happened to me?"

He responded, "This is that! This is that that was spoken by the prophet Joel: 'That I will pour out my spirit upon all flesh; and your sons and your daughters shall prophesy'." Newt rejoiced, "Beulah, this is what I have been telling you about. This is the Holy Ghost! You have received the Holy Ghost."

Very soon, the same poor, precious preachers and saints were visiting Bud and Beulah's home. They were now her brothers and sisters in the Lord and she had a new appreciation and understanding that they had forsaken all to preach the glad tidings and counted them among the faithful "of whom the world was not worthy."

I was a single man at that time (22 years old). My wife also attended the same meeting and received the Holy Ghost too. We later became acquainted and were married in the year of 1916 in the month of May. I was already preaching at that time so together we worked for the Lord. We held many revivals and saw many people come to God, repenting of their sins and receiving the Holy Ghost.

Newt always said that he "stole his wife". Newt's older sister, Eliza, had been married to Frank Flowers for ten years and he was well acquainted with the Flowers family. Frank had a younger sister named Elver. She was born on April 12, 1900. Elver was only sixteen years old and, although, her parents liked Newt, they felt that she was too young to marry. Newt was holding a revival at Trenton on May 27, 1916, the day that he and Elver slipped away from the revival meeting and were married.

Friends of Newt's teased him by saying, "Newt, you have been preaching a life free from sin. You have been telling everyone to stop stealing and now you have stolen your wife."

Newt laughed and said, "The Bible says to go and sin no more. I am not going to steal again."

I baptized literally hundreds of people in the name of Jesus Christ.

Newt heard the Jesus' name message preached at Jackson, Tennessee, and after careful study of the Bible and Acts 2:38, he was convinced that it was the truth. He and Elver were baptized in the precious name of Jesus Christ.

There was much division among the brethren concerning the "new issue". Brother W.M. "Billy" Mills, who had, together with Brother E.J. Douglas, brought the Holy Ghost message to Trenton, Tennessee, did not receive the message of Jesus' name baptism and they broke fellowship over the doctrine. At the time of the split, Brother Mills said that the Lord gave him Brother Douglas as a fellow laborer, a son in the gospel, and that he was a great preacher and a fine singer. He said that later the Lord gave him Brother Newt Graves and that he was fully as capable as Brother Douglas, but that the devil got both of them. The rift brought great pain and hard feelings on both sides.

At this time, Brother Newt Graves developed a growth on his hand. It was red, painful and cancerous in appearance. He had sought the Lord for healing of the lesion and it was not improved. One day as he walked down a street in Trenton, he passed through an alley that ran beside Brother Mills' house and, unexpectedly, met Brother Mills who was standing in his yard. They exchanged greetings and Brother Mills came to the fence and as they made small talk, Brother Mills noticed the growth on

Newt's hand. He said, "Brother Graves, what is that on your hand?"

Brother Newt said, "I don't know, it is causing me trouble."

Brother Mills said, "Let's pray and ask the Lord to take care of it." Brother Mills reached across the fence and covered the lesion with his hand. They both prayed and called upon the name of the Lord. When Brother Mills removed his hand from Brother Graves' hand, the lesion was gone. After all the hard words that had been spoken and the breach of fellowship, the Lord saw fit to minister healing.

During a revival in Trenton, Brother Newt Graves announced that there would be a baptismal service the next day on Sunday afternoon. The Jesus' name message was still new and many ministers had not decided where they stood on the issue. Brother Graves and Brother Paul Joyner, a dentist from Union City, Tennessee, were preaching the revival together, and they never knew who would be preaching until during the service the Lord would impress upon them who the speaker would be. Brother Graves had been baptized in Jesus' name, but Brother Joyner had not and was baptized in the titles: the Father, Son and Holy Ghost.

When it came time for the message to be preached on Sunday morning, Brother Graves walked over to Brother Joyner, handed him his Bible and announced to the congregation that Brother Joyner would be preaching the baptismal message. Brother Joyner protested and said, "No, no, you preach it." Brother Graves insisted that he preach. Beulah Graves, who was present that morning, said that she never heard a more anointed explanation of Jesus' name baptism at any time in her life, than Brother Joyner preached that day in 1916.

They went to a nearby lake, which is presently located at the intersection of the Trenton Bypass and the Milan Highway, across from the Trenton Sale Barn. The outline of the bank is still there today, though at that time it was a large man-made lake. Brother Newt Graves baptized Brother Paul Joyner in the name of Jesus Christ, and then they baptized the rest of the persons who presented for baptism. Brother Newt's father, mother and all his living siblings and their spouses were baptized in Jesus' name that day. They were: His parents: George Brown Graves and Caroline Whitwell Graves; his siblings and their spouses: Rev. William Pitts Graves and his wife, Bernice Skipper Graves; Frank M. Flowers and his wife, Eliza Graves Flowers; Rev. Sam Graves and his wife, Minnie Graves Graves; Addison Dickson "Bud" Graves and his wife, Beulah Walker Graves; and Willie H. Brown and his wife, Jimmie Graves Brown. (A sister, Ida, had died March 3, 1899 and a sister, Mattie, had died March 16, 1911.) They baptized couples together. Brother Newt Graves would baptize one spouse and Brother Joyner would baptize the other; they put them under the water at the same time.

Probably others were baptized on this occasion, but of these the author is certain, having been told countless times of the first Jesus' name baptism in Gibson County, Tennessee.

We saw many healed by the power of the Lord.

Addison Dickson "Bud" Graves, brother of Newt Graves, had the flu and lay dying in his parents' home. His mother and Newt opened the door to his bedroom and he became aware of their presence. His mother walked into the room and Newt followed her. As they entered the room, Bud became aware of a third person. A man followed Newt into the room and when Newt took a step, the man took a step; they moved in tandem.

Newt and his mother had come to lay hands on Bud and to pray for the Lord to heal his body and to spare his life. Bud lay in a four-poster bed which was pulled out away from the wall of the room, which allowed Newt to walk to the head of the bed with the man following closely. Bud stated later that when Newt stretched out his hand, the man stretched out his hand and touched him. He said that the man's touch was as soft as a mother's touch.

Bud's fever broke immediately. He began to perspire profusely, necessitating the changing of the bed-sheets. In a short time, Bud walked to the staircase and called downstairs to his wife and mother that he was hungry and wanted to eat.

We helped establish quite a few churches, some in Tennessee, some in other states during our early ministry.

Brother Newt Graves was at his father's house, outside Trenton, when the Lord spoke to him and told him to go to Paducah, Kentucky. He thought to himself, "I don't know anything about Paducah, Kentucky. I've never been to Paducah and I don't know anybody who lives there."

Newt had less than a dollar; but began to pack his clothes and get ready to go. He prayed, "Lord, if You will make a way, I will go."

He slept little that night and awoke with a heavy burden and clear impression that he should go to Paducah, Kentucky. He walked about one and one-half miles into Trenton and stopped by the local shoe store that was owned by Brother Westbrooks.

Brother Westbrooks said, "Well, bless the Lord, Brother Graves. What are you doing in town so early?"

Brother Graves said, "I am going to Paducah, Kentucky."

Brother Westbrooks said, "Well, bless the Lord! I've got a sister who lives there and, if you don't mind, I'll go with you."

Brother Graves assured him that he would be glad to have him go along.

Brother Westbrooks went home and quickly gathered a few belongings. He and Newt walked to the depot. Newt was praying inwardly all the way. When they reached the depot, Brother Westbrooks said, "Let's get our tickets."

Newt said, "There's plenty of time. No need to rush." He continued praying.

Brother Westbrooks again said, "Brother Graves, we need to get our tickets. We are going to miss the train."

Newt looked up and saw a man that he knew walking very rapidly toward the depot. The man walked straight to him and said, "Brother Graves, the Lord told me to give you this money." He gave five dollars to Newt.

Newt thanked the man and turning to Brother Westbrooks said, "Brother Westbrooks, let's get our tickets! We don't want to miss the train."

In Paducah, Brother Westbrooks' sister received the word gladly. She invited her friends and neighbors to her home for service and Brother Newt Graves preached the first Jesus' name message that was ever preached in Paducah, Kentucky that day. Several people received the Holy Ghost and were baptized in Jesus' name during the few days that he and Brother Westbrooks were there.

Brother Westbrooks said, "Brother Graves, I have another sister who lives in Dyersburg, Tennessee. I would like for you to go with me to talk to her about the Lord."

Brother Newt and Brother Westbrooks traveled to Dyersburg and the same thing happened there that had happened in Paducah. Brother Westbrooks' sister was converted and invited her friends and neighbors to her house for service. Brother Newt Graves preached the first Jesus' name message that was ever preached in Dyersburg, Tennessee, that day. A church was later established in Dyersburg as a result of their trip.

Brother Newt Graves held many revivals in homes, rented halls, brush arbors and had a tent at one time. Huge crowds were common. People came by horse and buggies or wagons.

He and Brother Sam Graves held a tent revival at Frog Jump, Tennessee, and many people from Frog Jump and the Old Quincy communities came out to hear and see the Pentecostals sing, preach and pray. During the service, someone shot several shots from a pistol. The crowd scattered. Sister Elver, Sister Minnie and Sister Beulah Graves and all the other mothers snatched up their babies from the pallets where they lay sleeping. The shooter didn't hit anybody and probably only wanted to cause a disturbance. Pioneer preachers were tough; they had to be.

We had three precious girls born into our family. They are all living today, for which we are thankful.

Brother and Sister Graves' daughters were Mary Voncille, Christine and Juanita.

When the children became of school age we began pastoral work. We pastored at Darden, Beacon, Scotts Hill, Adamsville, Hohenwald and Parsons, Tennessee.

Brother Newt Graves pastored six churches at one time. He did this by the circuit method, by having service on different days of the week at a different church each day until he had completed the circuit. These churches were Darden, Beacon, Scotts Hill, Adamsville, Hohenwald and Parsons, Tennessee. They met together in rented halls, homes, etc.

Darden was his main church for many years. Sister Nina King Benson, the wife of Rev. L. H. Benson, said that

Brother Newt Graves was her pastor throughout her growing up years.

Brother Graves later moved to Parsons and while the pastor of the church there, was also employed for more than twenty years as a state conservation officer for Decatur County. He developed a personal friendship with Tennessee Governor Frank Clement during this time, that later was a great blessing to the Tennessee District United Pentecostal Church.

We gave up the church in Parsons in 1950 and helped to build our campground at Perryville, Tennessee.

Rev. W. M. Greer wrote in an obituary of Rev. A.N. Graves: "His great love was for the Tennessee District and especially the District Camp Ground at Perryville. Brother Graves was very active in establishing the Camp Grounds and became the first custodian after it was developed until he left to establish a work in Memphis on Jackson Avenue which is now Bethel United Pentecostal Church."

After much progress had been made on the building of the District Camp Ground, Governor Frank Clement sent machinery and a crew of men to blacktop the roads at the campground. The governor's act of kindness was largely attributed to his friendship with Brother Graves.

In 1956 we left the campground and went to Memphis, and with the help of a few faithful people opened a church on Jackson Avenue. We labored there about three years. Our health failed and we had to give up the church. Rev. James Boutwell accepted the church and has done a very commendable job. The church is growing under his leadership for which we are very thankful.

We covet an interest in your prayers.

In 1956, at the age of sixty-three years, Brother A.N. Graves moved to Memphis to start what was to be his last church. Many of the saints in the church were from Darden,

Tennessee, who had moved to Memphis to find work. They named the church Bethel United Pentecostal Church, and the church continues today at a new location.

In 1956, Brother Graves health failed, and he and Sister Graves moved back to Perryville, where they purchased a home on property adjoining the District Camp Grounds. They lived happily there until the death of Sister Elver Graves on November 29, 1972. Brother Graves moved to Memphis to live with one of his daughters, where he died on April 10, 1974. He was eighty-one years old.

Rev. W. M. Greer wrote in an obituary published in the Tennessee Voice: "He was one of the closest friends this writer had, and he will be sorely missed by the entire district where he served as an honorary member of the board until his death.

The funeral was held in the Parsons Church which he helped to establish and served as pastor for several years.

A large group of friends and ministers were present to pay final tribute to a great man of God.

Ministers having a part in the funeral services were Rev. James Boutwell, District Home Missions Director, Nashville; Rev. L. H. Benson, District Sunday School Director, Nashville; Rev. W. M. Greer, District Superintendent, Jackson; Rev. E. E. Thomas, District Foreign Missions Director and pastor of Bethel Church founded by Brother Graves.

He was laid to rest beside his wife of more than a half century in the quiet countryside of his home county in Mount Tabor cemetery."

The humble beginnings on Jackson Avenue in Memphis of what later became Bethel United Pentecostal Church, and is now known as Bethel Church Ministries of Bartlett in the Memphis area. This was one of the visions brought to birth by the late Bro. Newt Graves.

Tennessee District Heritage 181

Rev. & Mrs. A.N. Graves

(Below) Bros. A.N. & Pitts Braves in 1956

Rev. A.N. Graves with his sixteen-year-old bride Elver, with whom he shared more than half a century.

MARVIN H. HANSFORD
By Harold Jaco, Jr.

February 10, 1912 was a day just like all others. There were children playing, parents working, people packing wood in their heaters to keep warm.

In eastern Arkansas, near the fabled "Hot Springs" which brought people from all around the world to bathe in their ostensibly healing flow, a little baby was born. Little did the parents, nor the city, nor even the imps of hell know the impact this child would have on the work of the Lord when his mother first took him in her warm and tender hands and loved her child. Proudly she spoke a name which would be comfort and inspiration to thousands during the next seventy-six years: Marvin Harold Hansford. Like all parents, Joseph and Laura Hansford were so proud of their baby boy. Eight years later a brother, James, completed the little family. Later, in a tragic railroad accident, Joseph Hansford, Marvin's father, was killed.

In 1929, young Marvin, now seventeen years old, surrendered his life to the Lord and felt the joy of full salvation in a meeting conducted by Reverend C. P. Kilgore, father of Reverend James Kilgore. He repented of his sins, was baptized by immersion in the precious name of Jesus Christ, and received the wonderful gift of the Holy Ghost. Two years later, at the age of nineteen, Marvin felt his call into the ministry. After a brief period of preparation, he launched out into his preaching ministry in 1932.

Also in 1932, Brother Hansford attended the General Conference of the Pentecostal Church, Inc. (predecessor to the United Pentecostal Church, International) which was held in Little Rock, Arkansas. During the Conference Brother Hansford met a young lady who captured his attention and held it for the next fifty-six years. The only daughter of Reverend Grover C. McDaniel, Catherine, was the lady of his dreams.

For four years he evangelized, preaching itinerately in revivals and crusades as the opportunities became available. During this time he was asked to fill in for Brother Grover McDaniel at the First Pentecostal Church of Pine Bluff, Arkansas. Brother McDaniel had taken sick and needed time for recovery. This was his first taste of pastoral ministry. He served for nine months. While there, his affection for Catherine became strong enough that he proposed marriage, and she accepted. On August 8, 1934, he was married to Miss Catherine Clair McDaniel. The following article was taken from the newspaper ...

Weddings
* * * * * * * *

McDaniel-Hansford

The marriage of Miss Catherine Clair McDaniel to the Rev. Marvin Harold Hansford which was solemnized Wednesday afternoon, August 8, in Pine Bluff at the home of the bride's brother, Ramond McDaniel, on South Poplar Street has been announced by the bride's parents, the Rev. and Mrs. Grover C. McDaniel.

The service was read at 6 o'clock in the afternoon by the bride's father, pastor of the Pentecostal Church of Louisisana, MO, at an improvised altar formed of ferns and lighted with white candles.

The house was decorated with choice summer flowers and greenery. Only members of the immediate families were present.

The bride's wedding dress was a pretty model in pink crepe with white accessories. Mrs. Hansford, an attractive brunette, is the only daughter of the Rev. and Mrs. McDaniel, and is a graduate of the local high school.

The bridegroom is the eldest son of Mrs. P. R. Hansford of Hot Springs and is a young minister of splendid ability. He is a graduate of the Hot Springs High School.

An informal reception for the wedding guests was held immediately following the ceremony.

In November 1934, Bro. Hansford was elected pastor in Clarksville, Missouri. He served the Clarksville church for only six months, and then moved on in May 1935 to serve a church in East Alton, Illinois. In 1936 the Hansford's moved to McClure, Illinois where they served that congregation for just less than five years. At Thanksgiving time in November 1939, as the nation was stumbling toward engagement in World War II, Brother Hansford accepted the challenge of the church in Iuka, Mississippi, where he served as pastor for two years. In 1941, he felt the call of God to go to Armory, Mississippi and begin a Home Mission work. The great church in Armory continues to serve this rural Mississippi Community even today. Reverend Coy Hill is the present pastor there. Remaining in Armory for two years, he was able to leave a church "on its feet" and poised to grow.

Later, in April 1943, the Hansford's moved to Laurel, Mississippi and pastored the First Pentecostal Church. For fifteen and one-half years he labored in this southern Mississippi town, building a strong congregation. Members of the Laurel congregation often expressed their confidence in this man of God, and were deeply moved when he reported the Lord was moving them on to Memphis, Tennessee.

While serving the Laurel church, Brother Hansford undertook an additional monumental task. The burden of Brother T. C. Montgomery had come to fruition with the development of the Tupelo Children's Mansion. Brother J. E. Ross, from Camden, Tennessee, built the first two buildings of the Mansion Campus. Brother Montgomery and Brother Hansford had together waded high weeds on the land which now is the spacious campus of TCM. In 1950, Brother Hansford was asked to serve in an interim capacity as the very first Superintendent of the Tupelo Children's Mansion until a successor could be elected. He spent about a year serving both as pastor at Laurel and Superintendent at Tupelo. He turned the responsibility of the Mansion over to Reverend and Mrs. L. J. Hosch, who were elected to serve.

During nearly twenty years of ministry in Mississippi, Brother Hansford served faithfully on the District Board, as District Secretary and as District Superintendent. (Brother Hansford served as District Secretary, then was elected District Superintendent, serving two years in that capacity, then was re-elected as District Secretary, and served until he moved to Tennessee.) Quoting from the July 1959 issue of the Mississippi District News, "This man's influence has been a great factor in the growth of the Mississippi District as well as the institutions that are located within its boundaries. Brother Hansford has served the Pentecostal Bible Institute and the Tupelo Children's Mansion since they were founded, as a member of their Executive Boards. The united best wishes from the entire Mississippi District go to our good friend and brother, Reverend M. H. Hansford, as he leaves our district and our prayers are for him to succeed in his new place of labor."

In 1958, Brother and Sister Hansford moved to Memphis, Tennessee to begin a rich ministry to the Calvary United Pentecostal Church. Due to the urban renewal project in Memphis at the time, the old location of the Calvary church was purchased and demolished at 120 E. Parkway North. The church moved to a new and much improved location at the corner of North Parkway and Dunlap as it reached out to the city of Memphis. Working with Brother Hansford in the music ministry was the talented Verle Pilant, who with his equally talented wife, Margie, gave a very special touch to the musical program.

One characteristic of M. H. Hansford was his ability to build a church staff of quality people. He surrounded himself with high caliber people to serve in various capacities. Names like Bob and Christine Lamply, Loren and Billy Beaty, Ruth and Dugan Cook, Duayen Tidwell, Butch and Sue Evans, and Jack and Ruth Holt, as well as many others, were his co-workers. He had a vision for growth and development. He was unwilling to allow the church program to "run itself" and just happen. Instead, he was pressing forward at all times with a quality effort to develop the work of God to its fullest! He was described by one person as being "Stately, Considerate, Compassionate, Gentleman, A Man of God, A Christian." In everything from the stationary on which he wrote his letters, to intercession in the prayer room, these qualities could be observed in this great gentleman.

Long before anyone knew anything about the current Home Missions program of Mother/Daughter Church Planting, Brother Hansford pioneered the effort. Brother Vondas Smith, who later became a Missionary to Bolivia, felt the call to begin a new work in Whitehaven a southern suburb of Memphis. When he approached Brother Hansford about the calling, Brother Hansford gathered together all the people from that area who attended his church and asked them if they would like to go and be a part of developing a church in the Whitehaven area. In one night service, Brother Hansford and Brother W. M. Greer commissioned some 20 people to leave the Calvary Church and go to help Brother Vondas Smith begin the Whitehaven United Pentecostal Church. That church grew and developed and is now one of the largest congregations in the Tennessee District United Pentecostal Church. It is currently known as The Pentecostal Church of Memphis. In its infancy, and for the first entire year, the Calvary church provided the rent and utilities to get the church started.

Soon after he had arrived in Memphis, he was elected to serve on the District Board as presbyter of what was then Section 7. Then only a few months later the brethren of the Tennessee District prevailed upon Brother Hansford to serve them as District Secretary. Being elected in 1959, he served continuously until his retirement in April 1980. In all, he served the Calvary Church for some eight and one-half years.

When the load of his Pastoral Ministry and that of District Secretary became too much, Brother Hansford felt the Lord lead him to resign Calvary UPC in Memphis. On June 7, 1967, Brother Hansford moved to the First Pentecostal Church on Lexington Avenue in Jackson, Tennessee as their new pastor. A number of people are still around who were a part of that congregation. Claude Vantreese was the song director. Family names such as Estes, Witherspoon, Fullington, Gilliam, Brickey, Bridger, Kemp, Bryant, Kuykendall, Lester, Johnson, Victory and a host of others were part of the congregation he served in Jackson for five years before the District asked him to give his full time to the office of District Secretary.

In January 1972, the District Board asked Brother Hansford to resign from his pastoral ministry and serve full time as District Secretary. This was a big step for the Hansford's, but after a time of prayer and consideration, he saw that this was the will of God and made the step of faith. Having to move from the parsonage of the First Pentecostal Church, a comfortable home on Russell Road, he and Sister

Hansford purchased the lovely house where she still lives at 26 Pecan Circle in South Jackson.

Across the street from the Bemis Pentecostal Church on Morton Street is a small building on the back lot of a residential house. At one time that building served as the Tennessee District Office of the United Pentecostal Church. In that building, Brother W. M. Greer, District Superintendent, and Brother M H. Hansford shared one desk on which to do the work of the District. Later on, Brother Hansford began writing checks to the builders who built the present District Office for the Tennessee District at 31 Harts Bridge Road. The receipts from the construction of that building are all still on file, many with the neat flowing handwriting of M. H. Hansford on them.

As District Secretary, Brother Hansford was instrumental in developing several improvements in the accounting system of the Tennessee District. His stamp is on many of the official records of the District. The desk he first used for the District is still on display at the District Office in the Historical Room, along with a number of other interesting exhibits concerning the life and ministry of this great man of God.

During his full time service to the Tennessee District, Brother and Sister Hansford served as Interim Pastor to a number of congregations in the Tennessee District. Among them are the Bemis Pentecostal Church and the East Dyersburg Pentecostal Church. His name is revered by those whom he served during those brief pastoral periods where he was able to hold churches together in the absence of a permanent pastor. Brothers Wendell Walker, Burley Flatt and Boss Lee of the East Dyersburg Church spoke of the wonderful stability of the church during the pastoral vacancy of about nine months, when the Hansford's faithfully drove up every Sunday to serve the church. Sister Flatt still today tells of the meals they shared together when Brother Hansford demonstrated how much he liked her "million dollar pie;" and the afternoons when the Hansford's would rest in their spare bedroom before the evening service. Many a church has been "held together" by the solid spiritual leadership which he gave them under these circumstances.

After his retirement, having served the Tennessee District as Secretary for more than 21 years, Brother Hansford continued his ministry with itinerate preaching engagements wherever and whenever needed. He kept up this pace until his health began to fail. Finally, on June 1, 1988, the Lord called Brother Hansford to that home He had been preparing for him for so long. If the devil had known back in February of 1912 how profitable this man's life would be to the work of the Lord, he would have trembled at the thought!

During 56 years of Apostolic Ministry, Brother Hansford spent more than 50 of those years in almost continuous service to the Church in one official capacity or another. Note this list of places of service. In Illinois he served on the District Board. In Mississippi he served on the District Board, as District Secretary, and District Superintendent. In Tennessee he served on the District Board and as District Secretary. Nationally, Brother Hansford served for ten years on the Board of Christian Education, both as Secretary and as Chairman. He served the Tupelo Children's Mansion on the Board of Directors, the Long Range Planning Committee, the Honorary Board and as Interim Superintendent.

At the funeral of M. H. Hansford he was surrounded by some of his closest friends and those who loved him dearly. Participating in the funeral at the Bemis Pentecostal Church were Horace Simmons and Marilyn Thomason in charge of the music, with singing by the Harmony Girls Trio, Janet Roberts, and Rev. L. H. Hardwick. Scripture and prayer were offered by Rev. Wayne Chester, District Secretary, and eulogizing comments were offered by Reverend W. M. Greer, District Superintendent Emeritus, Reverend L. H. Benson, District Superintendent, and

Reverend Stephen Drury, Superintendent of the Tupelo Children's Mansion. The funeral message was offered by Reverend Bill Luther, Pastor of the Bemis Pentecostal Church. Following the service, Brother Hansford was laid to rest in the Highland Memorial Gardens in Jackson, Tennessee. One comment made by Reverend W. M. Greer seems to sum things up for everyone: "No man is indispensable; but some men are irreplaceable."

The following memorial was published in the Pentecostal Herald concerning the life and ministry of Brother Hansford ...

MEMORIALS
M. H. Hansford

Reverend M. H. Hansford passed from this life on June 1, 1988. Brother Hansford was the retired secretary-treasurer of the Tennessee District.

Brother Hansford was born in Malvern, Arkansas, began his career in the ministry at age twenty. He pastored, churches in Clarksville, Missouri; East Alton and McClure, Illinois, Iuka, Armory and Laurel, Mississippi; and Memphis and Jackson, Tennessee. He served as the secretary-treasurer of the Tennessee District for twenty-one years. He also served as presbyter and director of missions. He was a former director and an honorary member of the Board of Directors of Tupelo Children's Mansion. After he retired from active ministry, he was a member of the Bemis Pentecostal Church, where he served on the Board of Elders and taught an adult Sunday School class.

> Brother Hansford leaves his wife, Catherine McDaniel Hansford, whom he married on August 8, 1934.

Ten years after his decease, a considerable honor was conveyed upon Brother Hansford posthumously by the Tupelo Children's Mansion. The following article is from the *Pentecostal VOICE of Tennessee,* May 1998 ...

Honor Bestowed on Rev. M. H. Hansford

During the Board Meetings at the Tupelo Children's Mansion in February 1998, a very special honor was conveyed upon Bro. M. H. Hansford. The Administration Building on the Campus was named the "M. H. Hansford Administration Building."

Bro. Hansford and his widow, Sis. Catherine Hansford, were life-long supporters of the Mansion. Indeed, Bro. Hansford was the very first Superintendent of TCM back during its first year of existence. Bro. Hansford worked hand-in-hand with Bro. T. C. Montgomery to help bring the Mansion from a dream to a functioning reality.

From its humble beginnings, TCM has grown into a thriving campus with nearly 30 buildings. Scarcely would it have been possible to envision the special effect the Mansion has had on the lives of numerous young people who have been privileged to have Mansion Parents.

Bro. Hansford was a member of the TCM Board from its beginning to the conclusion of his life. He was a part of the decisions and developments of the properties and staff. Nothing can be done at TCM which is not in some way affected by the gentle presence of this man of God who so loved the work of the Mansion.

How very fitting that the Administration Building should be named in his honor. Sis. Hansford, we salute you for the things you have given to our special children of the United Pentecostal Church from around the world.

In the *Pentecostal VOICE of Tennessee* for years there was a column entitled "From the Secretary's Desk – by Rev. M. H. Hansford." The following, and concluding passage is a quotation from the September, 1970 issue of the *VOICE* ...

The beautiful story recorded in Acts 3:1-8 contains one of the most blessed lessons one can learn. Peter and John truly found out that "It is more blessed to give than receive." They had been taught this truth through their association with Christ, but now they had experienced it in their own ministry.

The truth is obvious that we really only possess that which we give away. We are stewards of this life and its possessions. These become valuable only as we use them for God's glory. When Peter and John had prayed for the lame man and he was healed, he went immediately into the temple, leaping and praising God!

Methuselah lived nine hundred and sixty-nine years, but the Bible sums up his life in three short verses. There is no merit in living a long time unless we do something worthwhile with that time which has been allotted us. One day when Edward VII was Prince of Wales he was taking a ride, and an old woman, poor, ragged and hungry, not knowing who he was came up to his carriage and asked for help. Reaching down in his pocket he said, "I will give you a picture of my mother." The woman was greatly surprised when he drew out a gold coin, stamped with the image of Queen Victoria, and gave it to her.

We may not be able to give a large amount of money but such as we have we should give. God does not require the unreasonable, only that which we have in our possession. Christ said, "Freely ye have received, freely give." He also said, "With the same measure ye have measured to others, it shall be measured to you again."

Not only was Rev. M. H. Hansford a competent and dignified District Secretary for Tennessee from 1959-1980, he was also a great preacher of the Word of God!

Brother Hansford had such a unique and clear way of presenting the Gospel that he was a favorite speaker in many church anniversaries, homecomings, and other special services. In addition, he was a very successful interim pastor, filling in when church vacancies came. Many is the church which was blessed by his kind and wonderful ministry.

Enjoy that bite, Bro. Hansford! It took you fifty years of marriage to get to that bite of cake. Bro. and Sister Hansford were celebrating their fiftieth wedding anniversary in August of 1984.

R. G. JACKSON
By Flora Jackson, wife, and Mary Jackson

Roy Gordon Jackson, born March 14, 1918 in Henderson County, Tennessee, tenth child of Madison Troy (Doc) and Martha Elizabeth Stewart Jackson.

The family moved to Madison County in 1920, and R. G. received his early education at Lesters Chapel and Bemis Elementary Schools. His mother was invited to the Pentecostal Church by a neighbor, Mrs. Fannie Branch. She repented, was baptized in Jesus Name and received the Holy Ghost and led her family to the Lord. In a tent meeting on Colorado Street in Bemis where Rev. A. D. Gurley was pastor and evangelist, R. G. and three of his brothers repented. These four and 63 others were baptized in this revival. Thirty or more received the Holy Ghost.

On June 20, 1935. R. G. married Flora McNatt. They made their home in the rural area of Madison County until he went to work in the Bemis Cotton Mill. Their daughter, Ruth, was born just before they moved into the town of Bemis, Tennessee on Old Kentucky Street. It was there in their home that he received the Holy Ghost on July 11, 1937. Roy Joseph, their son, was born in Bemis.

Brother Jackson's ministry started in 1937 while he worked at the Bemis Mill. He went out on the little porch at their home on Old Kentucky Street and was praying. The Lord spoke to him as in an audible voice and said, "Aren't' you going to preach my Word?" After that he went with Brothers Herbert Austin, W. M. Greer, Judson Ivy, and others to their appointments. He preached his first sermon at Ayers School House on August 7, 1938. His text was Romans 6:23. One lady, Irene Ayers Rolison's aunt, received the Holy Ghost and several came to the altar in repentance.

Brother Jackson's first pastoral effort was in Scotts Hill, Tennessee. He took two weeks off from his job at the Bemis Mill to hold the revival. God moved in a great way and the revival continued two more weeks. Thirty received the Holy Ghost. He pastored there for a while before going to Iuka, Mississippi in 1942. The church was small but grew to a nice congregation and many received the Holy Ghost. God began to lead him to go to Henderson, Tennessee where he began a new work in 1943. The first services were in an old beer hall next door to a poultry house. They borrowed school desks to sit on. From this humble beginning, a basement church was built on Highway 45. With a wonderful group of saints, God blessed and many repented and received the Holy Ghost. While in Tennessee he served on the District Board.

In 1946, the church in Corinth, Mississippi called him to pastor them. There the church grew and did well. From Corinth, he moved to Humboldt, Tennessee in May 1949 and served in a new work there. In 1950 the Hohenwald Church needed a pastor. He was called and felt this was another opportunity to serve. While pastoring in Hohenwald, their daughter, Ruth, married Jimmy C. Turnbow. Attendance records in Sunday School were set during that time that as far as is known have never been broken.

From Tennessee, Brother Jackson went to Murphysboro, Illinois for a pastorate of three years. His ministry reached into different areas. After leaving Illinois, he went to Theodore, Alabama for three years. He returned to Tennessee and pastored the Lexington Avenue Church in Jackson for two years. His ministry was mostly evangelistic and he evangelized for a time. He settled in Gulfport, Mississippi to pastor there from 1964 to 1971. While in Mississippi, he served on the Advisory Board of the Tupelo Bible School of Tupelo and was Sunday School Director of the Mississippi District for a while.

Back in Tennessee again Brother Jackson accepted the pastorate of Northside Pentecostal Church but left again to evangelize for five years. His passion was for winning souls. He never settled long in one place because his desire was to reach the lost more so than the role of pastor. His message was the simple anointed gospel of repentance, baptism in Jesus Name and receiving the Holy Ghost. Many souls were won during his revivals. For 44 years he carried on a radio ministry with support of individuals and from his own resources.

As his health was declining after seven years on the field, he took the church at Beacon, Tennessee. While there, he found he had an incurable condition which forced him into retirement. Returning to his roots, he bought a home in the Bemis Community where he lived until his death on April 11, 1995. He left behind his wife of almost 60 years and his children and grandchildren along with a host of those won to God under his ministry.

The R. G. Jackson Family: R.G. Jackson, Flora (wife), Ruth and Joe.

Rev. R. G. Jackson and his wife, Rev. Flora Jackson.

Tennessee District Heritage 199

This was a record-breaking Sunday at First Church of Hohenwald. Bro. R. G. Jackson was pastor, and O. W. Williams, evangelist, are pictured above with the Sunday School staff. The attendance on this Sunday was 271!

T. RICHARD REED
By Vernita C. Reed, Wife

Brother C. P. Kilgore, father of James Kilgore, pastored the First Pentecostal Church of Corning, Arkansas, when 15 year old Richard Reed prayed through in the open-air meeting he was preaching. "This was not a 'brush-arbor' meeting, for the brush was still on the trees!" was a remark oft repeated by Brother Reed in reference to the night he received the baptism of the Holy Ghost.

The ministry of Brother Reed began in 1929 when he became the pastor of the First Pentecostal Church in Corning, Arkansas. His eight years of pastoring in Corning included some unique experiences. Brother L. H. Benson, former superintendent of the Tennessee District, tells how Brother Reed carried him, a visiting young evangelist, on his shoulders across a swollen creek. While pastoring at Corning, his first church, he began his radio ministry. On July 7, 1934, he aired his first broadcast over KBTM, Paragould, Arkansas.

In 1936, Brother Reed was elected National President of the Pentecostal Gleaners, the Youth Department of the Pentecostal Church, Inc.

The First Pentecostal Church of Trumann, Arkansas called Brother Reed as pastor in 1937. While in Trumann, God gave Brother Reed a burden for Jonesboro where there was no church of our faith. The Bible Hour Tabernacle in Jonesboro, Arkansas was opened in 1942. It became the center of Brother Reed's radio work, the "Blessed Old Bible Hour." Stations KLCN in Blytheville, Arkansas and KLCN in West Memphis, Arkansas broadcast the "Blessed Old Bible Hour" over the next fifty years.

A dream come true for Brother Reed was when he took his first trip to the Holy Land in 1952. Over the years he conducted twelve tours, receiving one free trip, along with other tour hosts from the Ministry of Tourism of Israel. Some preachers enjoy fishing or playing golf for pastime. Brother Reed's "hobby" was taking a group of people to see the land where the Bible was written and to walk where Jesus walked.

The Arkansas District elected Brother Reed as District Superintendent in the Spring conference of 1953. During the six years he held this office, he engineered the relocation of the Arkansas District Campground from the top of Mt. Crest - a very inconvenient location with no modern facilities - to Redfield, near Pine Bluff, Arkansas. Some people who opposed this change, thought they would never be able to receive a "mountain-top" experience without being on top of the mountain. A visit to this modern facility today during Camp Meeting or a Women's Conference with two thousand women praising and worshipping the Lord would soon erase any doubt concerning this theory.

With a growing family, three sons born from 1952 to 1956, Brother Reed realized his duties as Superintendent demanded his being away from home and church too much of the time, so he resigned this position and his church. He accepted a call to Laurel, Mississippi to pastor the First

Pentecostal Church, for Brother M. H. Hansford, the pastor, was moving to Memphis to pastor Calvary United Pentecostal Church.

The Reed family and the church family welcomed their baby daughter born October 5, 1960.

A telephone call from Brother W. M. Greer, Tennessee District Superintendent, told Brother Reed of a church in Memphis in need of a pastor. Brother Reed's answer was "I'll pray about it." As he prayed, a burden for this need came to him. Thanksgiving holidays in 1962 found the Reeds moved to Memphis. The first order of business for the new pastor was to reorganize the church and relocate to a more desirable area. The First Pentecostal Church was now the First United Pentecostal Church at 1915 Young Avenue at Barksdale.

The Tennessee District elected Brother Reed as Presbyter in April 1968. He served the Memphis area as Presbyter for seventeen years and then was an "honorary member for life" of the district board. He also served as Harvestime representative for the district for a number of years. Editor of the Tennessee Voice, the district publication, was another position held by Brother Reed for a number of years.

Moving day for the church came, once again. An eight year old church in East Memphis, Mallory at Watson, was offered for sale by the pastor, J. H. Ford. The old church at Young and Barksdale was sold in an unbelievably short time. The newer church was bought in August of 1980. A Golden Jubilee celebration honoring Brother Reed for fifty years of continuous broadcasting the gospel was given by the church on July 21, 1984. The next day, the church celebrated its twenty-first anniversary. On December 30, 1984, Brother Reed resigned as pastor of First United Pentecostal Church, having suffered two strokes during the year. He continued to serve as pastor until the church elected a new pastor in March 1985. Brother James Sharp of Columbus, Ohio, was elected as the new pastor.

For the first time in fifty-six years, Brother Reed was free from the responsibility of pastoring. The desire to preach still burned within his heart. He prayed for open doors to minister and invitations came. The following year, he ministered in twenty-seven churches in Tennessee, Alabama and Arkansas.

As his wife, mother of his children, chauffeur, and secretary from 1944 until the Lord called him Home on March 16, 1993, I give God all the glory, honor and praise for any accomplishment during the sixty-plus years of ministry, both in the pulpit and over the airwaves, of this pioneer of the gospel.

Rev. T. Richard Reed and wife, Vernita C. Reed. Bro. Reed conducted a radio ministry for more than *Fifty Continuous Years!*

Below are Rev. & Mrs. T. R. Reed and Family in an early photo.

GLADYS ELIZABETH ROBINSON
By Mary Jackson
Information from daughter, Marie Wallace and
Nona Freeman's book "Box 44 Monrovia"

Gladys Elizabeth Cox was born May 17, 1907 in the rural community of Ozark, Illinois. She was the youngest of Betty Elizabeth and John Allan Cox's four children.

In 1924, at seventeen years of age she married her childhood sweetheart, Garrie Everett Ross. A daughter, Marie Evelyn was born on July 31, 1925. Before her only son, Allan Loree was born in 1927, the dream of "living happily ever after" dissolved, and Gladys was left along with two small children.

Gladys married Labon Carter Campbell in 1928. Carmen Elizabeth was born in 1930, bringing joy to this happy family. Carmen was only five years old when the death of Carter left Gladys again with shattered dreams and the great responsibility of three young children. With the help of a cousin, Anna, to care for the children, she worked at various jobs to keep her home together.

In 1939, she was married to Leo Robinson, a widower with three children, Jackie, Sue and Barbara. This marriage also proved to be a disappointment. In July 1940, Gladys attended a tent revival and made peace with God. A few days later Brother and Sister Raymond Yonts visited her and in a prayer meeting in a wooded area she received the wonderful gift of the Holy Ghost. With this gift came a wonderful vision of ministering in a land of mud huts. Brother Yonts baptized her in the name of the Lord Jesus. At that time, she confided in him that some day she would see this vision fulfilled of her reaching out to black women and naked babies. At first Leo made a move for God, but a short time later retreated and bowed out of her life amiably. He did not desire to walk with God but did not want to hinder her in the way she chose.

Sister Robinson moved to Nashville, Tennessee in June of 1942 and began worshipping in the church at 51st and Delaware Avenue. Her burning desire sent her out to reach the lost, often walking down streets giving out tracts. She taught the Berean Sunday School Class and held regular services at a nearby tuberculosis sanatorium. Her daughter, Marie, married Glenn Wallace on June 18, 1943.

In the summer of 1945, she returned to Ozark, Illinois and conducted a tent revival there. A number of people were converted and filled with the Holy Ghost. Sister Robinson established the United Pentecostal Church in that town and pastored there until God provided a way for her to attend the Apostolic College in Tulsa, Oklahoma in 1946, after she had been endorsed by the Missionary Board as an outgoing missionary to Africa.

On July 31, 1947, Sister Robinson left for Liberia, West Africa to assist Sister Georgia Regenhardt of Corinth, Mississippi at the Mahaeh Mission approximately 80 miles interior from Monrovia. They, along with several native workers, evangelized in some of the surrounding villages and tribes. Her presence and her burden for lost souls was a great help and blessing to the work in Africa.

The U. S. Steel Corporation of America made plans for a mining camp at Bomi Hills, in 1948, for the mining of iron ore. This was one of the villages to which the gospel had been carried by these missionaries. Sister Robinson wrote to Brother Wynn T. Stairs, Director of Foreign Missions, for permission to establish a day school and church at this location where representatives of many tribes would obtain employment and make their homes. Brother Stairs was so impressed with the opportunities offered at Bomi Hills that he felt to personally sponsor this endeavor until such time as missionary funds were available to take care of another mission. Sister Robinson then obtained permission from the Liberian Government and moved to a small mud hut in the village. Many other religious organizations were interested in establishing a work here, however, as long as one missionary was in the village, the government would not permit another organization to come in. Bomi Hills was to have the only road interior and the only railway from Monrovia. Ten or twelve native tribes were represented in this village as well as several Dutch families. The United Pentecostal Church was granted twelve and one-half acres of land for the establishing of the school and church. The mission has grown from the very beginning and many have received the Holy Ghost. Native workers have received proper training and teaching and have carried the gospel to members of their own tribes.

Sister Robinson spent three and one-half years of her first term in Liberia before returning to Nashville. During her one-year furlough, much of her time was spent visiting churches, conferences and gathering equipment for the work of the Bomi Hills Mission. She had very little time to be with her family, but it was her delight when Carmen and her husband, Norman, or Glenn and Marie could take her to services. Nearing the end of her deputation, another prayer was answered. Gene Bailey from Tulsa was appointed to Liberia. She would not return alone. God provided a helper!!

On March 18, 1952, they were brought home to the Bomi Hills Missions. By April, they settled into the familiar routine of teaching, overseeing buildings on the mission and treks into other villages to reach souls.

In early June, Gladys had so much pain in one leg that she gave in and went to the Dutch doctor who worked at the mine hospital. She was told she had a tumor and must return to the states for surgery. Her disappointment was so great that the doctor agreed to check her again in two weeks. The second examination showed no improvement and the doctor suspected malignancy and the mission officials ordered her home. She went, leaving her heart and most of her personal possessions, confident that she would soon return to Africa.

The doctor's suspicion was confirmed by surgery in America which revealed the fatal extent of the cancer invading her body. She found that even the darkest valley has a fragrant bloom or the ripple of a tiny refreshing stream. Gladys and Leo were not divorced. When he heard she was home ill, he came to be with her and renewed his vows to both her and the Lord. Their unexpected reunion, approved by those who loved her, brought a bitter-sweet happiness. They made plans, that if the miracle came, Leo would go with her to Africa. He could take over the building and repairs, and she would never again be alone on jungle trails. In the meantime, he was a constant friend and helper.

For a while she thought perhaps they might see this dream come true. Brother E. L. Freeman, another missionary to Africa, was on furlough and came to visit Gladys in November 1953. She spoke wistfully of the miracle that would let her return to Bomi Hills. There could have been one, for there have been many such miracles. But a month later, December 10, in one moment, inexorable pain traced its haggard etching on her face; the next moment, a valiant spirit took wings and in that split second, sudden glory illuminated with beauty that empty house of clay. Sister Robinson's hope to return to Africa to gather more "Jewels from the Jungles" ended as God called her home.

"Her work on earth is done, her life crown has been won and she is now at rest with Him above. Some glad morning she, I know, will welcome me to that Eternal Home of peace and love."

Gladys Robinson, July, 1947, prior to leaving for New York and Liberia, W Africa

Above, Gladys Robinson harvesting bananas with Sis. Georgia Regenhardt on November 2, 1947.

Left, Gladys Robinson on Nov. 27, 1947 with Sis. Pauline Gruse in Liberia. The "Trek to Buleswah".

W. A. SINGLETON
By Mary Jackson

William Alton Singleton was born December 18, 1903 in Henderson County, Tennessee. He moved to Bemis, Tennessee at an early age and went to work in the Bemis Cotton Mill. Here he met his future wife, Margaret E. Wyatt. She was originally from Decatur County which adjoins Henderson County where he was born, and they knew one another's families. They began dating and were married on October 25, 1929.

They began attending the Bemis Pentecostal Church and repented. Rev. A. D. Gurley baptized them in Jesus Name. Brother Singleton received the Holy Ghost in 1935. He acknowledged his call to preach and began preaching in 1937. Their first child, a girl named Bobbye, was born in 1930. Then a son, Joe, was born in 1932. Two girls, Carol and Ruth, were born in 1934 and 1936. To complete a wonderful family, God added another son, Dennis, in 1943.

Brother Singleton's desire to reach souls was great, and he started his first church, the Spring Hill Pentecostal Church, near Lexington in 1940. Later, the church moved across the highway and was called the Blue Goose United Pentecostal Church. In 1942, they moved to Iuka, Mississippi where he pastored for three years. He not only served the Iuka Church as pastor, but also on Sunday afternoon, he preached at another small church called Tobes Chapel. These were rough days for a young preacher with a family of seven to support. Sometimes his week's pay was only $10.00. Yet in answer to the prayers of Brother Singleton and his wife, money would come through the mail from someone the Lord impressed to send it. God did some wonderful things for this family.

Bobbye's eye was cut and the doctor said she would lose sight in it. Brother Singleton met Brother A. D. Gurley on the street and they had prayer for Bobbye. Her eye was healed. Another child, Carol, was bitten by a black widow spider and almost died. Again, they believed the Lord and she was healed.

From Iuka, they moved to Nashville, Tennessee in 1946 and attended the West Nashville Pentecostal Church pastored by Brother J. W. Wallace. Times were hard, so Brother Singleton went to work in the cotton mill in Nashville. His desire to preach was so strong, he would drive from Nashville to Blue Goose to minister every Sunday. Sometimes he would fall asleep driving. The family knew they had to stay awake to help keep him awake. During these years Brother Singleton was either building a church or helping to build one.

In 1949 the family moved back to Bemis. Brother Singleton again began work in the Bemis Cotton Mill and continued to preach at the Blue Goose Church. He resigned the Blue Goose church after a year or so and was elected pastor at Beauty Hill Pentecostal Church.

The children all married. Bobbye married Sammy Bond and moved to Counce, Tennessee. Joe married while in service and after his discharge he lived in Topeka, Kansas. He lived there until his death in 1990. Carol married James Dorris, and Ruth married Pete Pruitt. Both Carol and Ruth live in the Jackson area. Dennis and his wife live in Pensacola. Florida.

Brother Singleton was elected pastor at Parsons Pentecostal Church after leaving Beauty Hill. While pastoring at Parsons, he and Sister Singleton moved to the Pentecostal Camp Ground at Perryville, Tennessee. They continued to live there after resigning the Parsons church.

Eight years after moving away, they came back to the Bemis area to a lovely, little country home. He was an ardent gardener, and his children and grandchildren enjoyed the fruits of his labor. And they especially liked "grandma's" cooking. But not content to just garden, in 1978, he and Sister Singleton joined the group beginning a new church at 250 Chester Levee Road. When the group became the South Side United Pentecostal Church, Brother Singleton was chosen to minister to them. He blessed this congregation with his preaching, prayers and great faith until they elected Brother Hulon Myre as pastor. He continued to worship with them until he was again asked to come to Blue Goose as their pastor. At this time, his health was not good so he asked Rev. R. G. Jackson to assist him with the pastorate at Blue Goose. Both served for several months until he had to retire because of his health. He always had a special love for this church because it was his first church and he helped build the building.

He and Sister Singleton enjoyed over 60 years together. She passed away on January 16, 1992 of lung cancer. Following her death, his health deteriorated until he could no longer live alone. His last years were spent in Forest Cove Nursing Home where at age 90, he would still preach to anyone who would listen. He departed this life for his eternal reward on December 13, 1994.

212 Tennessee District Heritage

Pastor and Wife W. A. Singleton at Parsons First Church with Rev. W. M. Greer "Burning The Note"!

Bro. Singleton's first church, before he left Bemis to go to Blue Goose: Joe, Bobbye, Ruth, Margaret, W. A., and Carol

(Right) Bro. Tyler, W. A Singleton, Minton Anderson, and Paul Price.

(Far Right) W. A. Singleton is pictured with his first automobile!

W. T. SCOTT
by Judy Bagsby, daughter

W. T. Scott was born February 7, 1910 in the Riverside Community of Lewis County near Hohenwald, Tennessee. He was the son of John and Josie Scott and the eldest of six children. One brother and one sister remain. He attended school in Lewis County and received further education at Watkins Institute in Nashville.

On October 4, 1922 at the age of 12, Brother Scott received the marvelous infilling of the Holy Ghost. He says this is and will always be the "RED LETTER DAY" of his life. No experience before or since that day comes even remotely close to the joy of receiving the Holy Ghost experience in his life. He regrets deeply the eight years of his life that he turned his back on the Lord during his twenties. Brother Scott says he felt the call of God to preach the Gospel almost as soon as he received the Holy Ghost. His family was attending church under the leadership of an early Pentecostal pioneer, Brother T. M. Frazier. Both of his parents also received the Holy Ghost during this time.

At the age of 18, Brother Scott became employed with Bell Telephone Company in the division office and later was a line foreman based in Nashville. He continued working with the telephone company for 18 years prior to entering the ministry. During this time, he met Hazel Marie Murphy of Tracy City, Tennessee. They were married on June 6, 1931 in Tracy City and settled in Nashville. Sister Scott was of another faith and very much against the Pentecostal message. Brother Scott says that after eight years of praying and fasting for his wife, she opened her heart and received this wonderful Holy Ghost experience in 1939. She was a devoted helpmate and supporter of the ministry from that day forward. She had a wonderful sense of humor and loved playing practical jokes – particularly on other pastors, evangelists, district superintendents. etc.

Brother and Sister Scott have three children. Jerry was born in 1941 and is now living in Gallatin; Judy was born in 1943 and now lifes in Dover; and the youngest, Charles (Red) was born in 1948 and is living in Murfreesboro. They have three grandchildren and five great-grandchildren.

After moving to Nashville, Brother Scott began attending a trinity Pentecostal church. Brother Scott explains that although this church did not have the truth of the "One God" message, he gives them credit for his having received some valuable teaching under their leadership. He pastored a small church in Gallatin, Tennessee and assisted at a church in Nashville prior to moving to Goodlettsville. Brother Scott became the pastor of Goodlettsville United Pentecostal Church in the mid-1940's and continued until 1967-68. In 1951 when the Tennessee District was divided into three sections, he was elected to serve as presbyter of the Eastern Section along with Bro. J. W. Wallace. He served in this office from 1951 – 1957 and again in 1961 until 1963. He has many wonderful stories to tell of his years as pastor and church leader. Several men received calls to the ministry under Brother Scott's leadership, and several churches were established as a branch from the Goodlettsville church.

Brother Scott is a tall, soft-spoken man who has a keen insight of the Bible and the truth of the "Mighty God in Christ." His theme has always been "Ye shall know the truth, and the truth shall make you free." He is now 89 years of age with an alert mind but weak in body and lives in an assisted living facility called Walking Horse Meadows, 207 Uffelmann Drive, #138, Clarksville, Tennessee 37040. He would love to hear from his friends and fellow ministers through visits, cards, letters, or phone calls. His telephone number is 931-906-5705. He also would appreciate your prayers.

Sister Scott suffers from Parkinson's Disease and is in McKendree Village, Inc., 4347 Lebanon Road, Room N155, Hermitage, Tennessee 37076. She too would appreciate your visits, cards and letters, and especially your prayers.

Bro. W. T. Scott in 1950

Happy Fiftieth Anniversary as the W. T. Scott Family celebrates together: June 16, 1981.

Biographies of Second and Third Superintendents and Report of Fiftieth Anniversary

LOWELL H. BENSON
By Mary Jackson

It was a cold night in December 1932 when Lowell Benson made his way to a little mission on South Broadway in St. Louis, Missouri. After hearing the message in song and sermon, he made his way to the altar and surrendered his empty and worthless life to God.

Having lost his parents by age 3, he was raised by grandparents until his mid-teens when his grandmother developed cancer and broke up housekeeping, leaving a teen-aged boy to his older sister who lived in St. Louis. But Brother Benson soon became restless, joined with an older man who was a professional hobo who taught him all the tricks of the trade. This was during the great depression. Jobs could not be found. Thirteen million people in America were out of a job and here is a kid, due to circumstances, with limited education, who did not fit into the mainstream of things. Restless, always on the move, riding freight trains from state to state until the night he attended services in the mission. That experience changed the life of the "hobo kid!"

The mission where he was converted was a trinity church, but Lowell had heard the Jesus Name message while living in the hills of Arkansas and insisted on finding a preacher who would baptize him in the Name of Jesus, and he is still just as strong on Jesus Name baptism now as he was then.

Lowell went over to Granite City, Illinois where Brother Odell Cagle was pastoring. Brother Cagle took him in and gave him a home. Within the same year, he felt his call to the ministry. When Brother Cagle left the church, Brother Benson was appointed interim pastor until Brother Ross Smith was elected pastor.

His first missionary journey was in 1933, when he and another young preacher "hitch-hiked" from Granite City to southeast Missouri where they held a revival in a schoolhouse until school started. Then the people built a brush arbor and the revival continued for six weeks. Sixty-two people were baptized in the wonderful name of Jesus!

Upon returning to the home church in Granite City, they talked to their pastor about leaving immediately on another preaching trip. Brother Benson had bought a 1927 Model T Ford on credit with no license plates. His traveling friend borrowed enough money from his brother-in-law to buy the license. So they were ready to travel with no destination in mind. Their pastor said to wait until the weekend, and we'll take an offering for you. Brother Benson's answer was, "Pastor, the Lord may come before the weekend. The world needs our message!" So they filled the gas tank, which was under the hood, right in front of the windshield with gas that cost them 12 cents a gallon and headed south. To hear Brother Benson tell it now, they were loaded with zeal but empty on wisdom!

In 1934, while helping Brother Cagle in revival in Finley and Dyersburg, Tennessee, he met Nina King. She was a beautiful young lady who attended the Finley Church. It was love at first sight, even though he was only 19 and she was 18. They were married on November 24, 1934.

For 65 years, they have worked together as a team to help reach their world for Christ.

Brother Benson was always looking for a place to preach. He would preach on street corners, brush arbors, court squares or any place where people would listen. Later he owned a tent and held tent meetings and started some churches under the old gospel tent. In 1935 and '36, jobs were still hard to find. He worked a number of jobs for $1.00 per day, but preaching always came first. In the fall of the year, he would go to southeast Missouri near Kennett and pick cotton. At the same time, he would get permission to hold a revival in a nearby schoolhouse. They picked cotton by hand in those days. After picking cotton all day, dragging a nine-foot cotton sack, he would preach every night. On Saturday, he would drive to Kennett and preach on the street. They did not stay in motels in those days. Many nights he slept on a blanket or quilt on the floor. These were lessons that later proved very helpful as he began pastoring.

Brother and Sister Benson have pioneered and built five churches. He has pastored a number of churches in Tennessee including Darden, Henry County Tabernacle, Oak Ridge, West Nashville and East Nashville. He also pastored in Sheffield and Pritchard, Alabama.

When Alabama became a District in 1949, Brother Benson was elected District Secretary. The following year, he was elected District Superintendent and served three years before resigning and returning to Tennessee to pioneer another church.

In 1958, Brother Benson was elected Sunday School Director of the Tennessee District. At the time of his taking this office, the Sunday School tithing program was not functioning efficiently, the results being a very small amount of funds in the treasury to operate the department.

Likewise, the reports of individual Sunday Schools were not being sent to the office. Brother Benson immediately launched a program to encourage more cooperation from our Sunday Schools. The District Board approved his plan, and an immediate response was received. The records show marked improvements in these areas.

One of the outstanding efforts at this time was the National Sunday School Convention held in the District in May of 1959. This brought many great teachers and Sunday School workers to the District. The Sunday School Department experienced rapid growth under the leadership of Brother Benson.

During the time Brother Benson was District Sunday School Director, he was full time pastor of churches in Nashville. He drove many miles in his ministry and Sunday School work and wore out a number of cars from a Fiat to Cadillacs. Much of his life has been spent in his car.

When Rev. W. M. Greer resigned in mid-term in 1978, Brother Benson was elected District Superintendent of Tennessee to finish the remaining term. In April 1979, he was re-elected to the office and served a total of 17 years always being elected on the nominating ballot. While he was District Superintendent, 135 new ministers were licensed and 22 new churches were added to the District. In his years, the program "Build A Church in a Day" was begun. A church at Sevierville and one at Dayton were built with this program.

He was superintendent when an era of Camp Meeting at Perryville ended. In 1987, the Camp Meeting was held in Jackson, Tennessee at the Civic Center. Youth Camps continued at "Holiness Hill" in Perryville until the campground was sold in 1993. A campsite was purchased at Bon Aqua, Tennessee, and Brother Benson with the

District Officials closed the deal on September 6, 1994. He resigned as District Superintendent in April 1995.

In summary, Brother Benson attended his first General Conference in 1935 and has only missed one from 1935 to 1994. He tells us, that one of the greatest honors bestowed upon him was when he was asked to preach at the General Conference in 1963.

He served for sixteen years on the National Sunday School Committee and twenty years on the General Board, a total of thirty-six years working directly with the national organization of the United Pentecostal Church. He made several trips abroad to preach in conferences and dedicate churches.

He and Sister Benson have lived a busy and rewarding life, but the most rewarding and the most fulfilling to them is when they are working and worshipping with the Tennessee family of God.

L. H. Benson, District Superintendent from 1978 – 1995.

Evangelist L. H. Benson and Singer George White

The Young Preacher Man, Rev. L. H. Benson

April, 1978, Bro. W. M. Greer passes the mantle of leadership to Bro. L. H. Benson, the Second District Superintendent of Tennessee

L. H. Benson: **STILL** a Travelin' Evangelist!

WAYNE CHESTER
Autobiography: 6-22-99

On the morning of October 9, 1932, the second child was born to Houston and Geraldene Chester, who lived in the hills of Benton County. The proud parents named him Gordon Wayne Chester. When I was born, I had a four-year-old sister, Mary Dean Chester. We lived in a little community named Dog Fork. I vividly recall playing in the dusty road that led from our little house to my uncle's house that was just down the road.

I enjoyed life as a young child, even though we were very poor. However, I didn't know we were poor! We lived in a small three-room house with no insulation, and a small tin heater to heat the house and big iron cook stove. I recall my father getting up when the air was so cold in the house that you could see your breath. He would put some wood and kindling in the tin heater along with some kerosene, and then we would enjoy the sound of that little heater as it almost danced off the floor. Our medical treatment usually consisted of rubbing our chests with Vicks salve and then wrapping a stove eye in cloth and putting it on our chests when we had a cold, or sometime Mom would give me that awful tasting stuff called black draught tea!

Ugh! Liquid cod liver oil was about as bad; castor oil was worse!

My grandfather, Bob Mays, on my mother's side lived just across the pasture. I enjoyed being with him. I recall him popping popcorn in the big fireplace in their house. He died at an early age. They did not take bodies to the funeral home in those days, but they just took down a bed, and the casket was placed in the room with the fireplace until time to take it to the church for the funeral. My grandmother, LeVada Mays, lived for many more years, reaching the age of 88.

My grandparents on my father's side died during the flu epidemic that swept the country just prior to my birth. They died three days apart.

I attended a small country school, called Morris Chapel. I have vivid memories of my early school days. I remember the smell of oil that they put on the floors to hold the dust down, bringing water from a well and having our little metal folding drinking cups, the school plays, and recess. Of course there were some unpleasant memories when we had to stick our heads under the table while the teacher proceeded to whack our backsides with a switch when we misbehaved. Our school bus consisted of a large old car owned by Miss Mattie Lashlee. Often there would be 15 or more kids crammed in that car when we first left the school.

My father worked at Memphis Stone and Gravel Company for several years. This was a very unhealthy place to work due to the dust that was in the air. When I was nine years old, he developed pneumonia, but didn't see a doctor right away as money was very scarce. His condition worsened and finally he was taken to the hospital in Paris, Tennessee. They were unable to do much for him, and he realized that he was going to die. He wanted to be taken home to die. My uncle, Bill Chester, had been building us a little house on the old home place in Morris Chapel, about four miles out of Camden, Tennessee. It was just a boxed house with a tin roof and no insulation. So my mother decided to bring my dad home, and he died the next day at the age of 36 years. Mother was now left with two children to raise with no income. There were no social programs back then to help those in need.

The Second World War was just getting underway. My mother's brother Claudie Mays had already taken his family to Detroit, Michigan to find work. They wrote to my mother and told her there was a little one room apartment at the back of their house that we could rent, and my mother could get a job in one of the factories there making airplanes. We boarded the Greyhound bus and headed for Detroit. We lived in a suburb of Detroit, called Melvindale. I attended grade school there but really did not like it, because they called me "Tennessee Slim" and a hillbilly.

After about three years we moved back to Tennessee and back to the old home place. I graduated from the 8th grade at Morris Chapel and then enrolled at Central High School in Camden, Tennessee. In the meantime, my mother had remarried. She married George A. Lewis. He treated me okay, but I was not too excited about a stepfather. After a few years, they had a child, my half-brother, Jerry Wilbur Lewis. I recall him watching for the school bus when I would come home in the afternoon, and he would run to meet me.

I became involved in sports while in high school. I made the football team all four years, but was more successful in the basketball program due to my height as I was now 6'5" tall. I had four successful years as a high school basketball player, which resulted in me being offered scholarships at several schools. Some of the schools that were interested in me were the University of Tennessee at

Knoxville, the University of Tennessee at Martin and Bethel College of McKenzie, Tennessee. I chose to attend Bethel College as I felt that going to a smaller school I would have the opportunity to play more, and it was also closer to home! While at Bethel, I was a starter all fours years, was captain two years and made the All State Team two years.

On the academic side, I made "Who's Who in American Colleges and Universities" my senior year. I had a double major in Health and Physical Education and Biology.

After graduation from college, I accepted a position as head coach in a little town in the "boot heel" of Missouri called Bell City. During the cotton season, they would dismiss school for about six weeks. As I did not have anything to do at this time, I would pick cotton. I became quite good at picking cotton, as I recall. One day I picked 600 pounds. While in Missouri I bought a restaurant. My mother moved there to help me manage the restaurant. We had living quarters there. I stayed there for three years and then was offered a job in my hometown as Athletic Director and head basketball coach. A new building had just been constructed, and I was excited to be going home.

I had a very successful tenure at Central High School in Camden, winning most of the games and having packed out crowds at every home game. During this time, I had one young man emerge by the name of Danny Boyd who was an outstanding basketball player. During his senior year he broke the state record for the number of points made in a single game scoring 104 points in a single game. That record still stands today. What makes this so outstanding is the fact that he sat out of the game for three minutes, and there were not any three point shots in those days.

But not only was he instrumental in my success as a basketball coach, but through him and his mother, I was introduced to Pentecost. I recall in my earlier years, my father taking the family to a "homecoming" at a Pentecostal Church near Camden, but I was not old enough to know much about what was going on.

Danny did not have any way to get home after basketball practice, therefore I would often take him home and became acquainted with his family. His mother was a member of the Rushings Chapel Pentecostal Church. She would invite me to attend their Sunday School, which I did attend a few times. It was in this Sunday School class that I met my wife to be, Carolyn Sue Wright.

Rev. Jimmy Meade was preaching a revival at the Rushings Chapel Pentecostal Church during the summer of 1961. I began to attend the revival services. The Lord began to deal with my soul, and I repented of my sins and was baptized in the Tennessee River by Brother Meade. I began to seek the baptism of the Holy Ghost. I received the Holy Ghost on a Sunday night at the First United Pentecostal Church in Camden. It was joy unspeakable and full of glory!

I had already signed a contract to coach another year, therefore I completed that year and then resigned my position as basketball coach. I went to Western Apostolic Bible College (now called Christian Life College) in Stockton, California. I taught in the high school department and attended as many college classes as I could, along with working at night in order to support myself.

At the end of the first semester, I came home and my wife and I were married at the Rushings Chapel Pentecostal Church by Rev. Jimmy Meade. Our honeymoon consisted of traveling back to California after the Christmas vacation. Our first home was a little tin building located on the campus. We had a small apartment on one side, and then the high school boys had the other side. We were blessed when we came back the next year because a trailer had been purchased for us to live in, which was a big step up from where we had been the year before. About a year later our first little girl came along, Sonna Lariece Chester.

At the end of that school year, we decided not to return to Stockton and find employment in Tennessee. I was able to secure a teaching position at Big Sandy School. We moved to Big Sandy and were able to rent a house for $35.00 per month. We lived in two new houses while in Big Sandy, and the most rent we paid was $45.00 per month! Things do change! I also was elected to my first pastorate of a little church near Holladay, Tennessee. I had some unique experiences there. For example, I had to teach Sunday School, take the offering, play the piano, and anything else that needed to be done. One time I stopped preaching, took Sonna out on the front porch and spanked her and then came back in and continued preaching.

At the end of my first year in Big Sandy, I was selected to be Principal of the school which was grades K-12. I enjoyed my stay in Big Sandy and remained there for nine years. During this time, I also was pastor of the Bruceton United Pentecostal Church.

Our second daughter, Tami Sue Chester, was born. We were a very happy family even though I thought Sonna and Tami would kill each other from time to time. We kept our daughters involved in the things going on in the District. Anytime there was a gathering of young people, we tried to have them there. We have never missed a Thanksgiving Youth Retreat since they began.

The First United Pentecostal Church of Camden elected me to serve as their pastor in 1969. The Lord blessed and we built a new church and a new parsonage on the ten acres of property that the church had purchased previously. When we went there the church was only supporting two foreign missionaries. I went to General Conference one year and took them all on, not knowing what kind of response I would get from the church body. But I have found out you can't outgive God. We then supported over 30 missionaries and the new church and new parsonage were completely paid for!

Our daughters, along with Larry Beasley and Dennis Watts formed a singing group called the "Conquerors." They sang at various events around the District. When I accepted the pastorate of the Camden church, I also resigned as principal of the big Sandy School and was elected to serve as vice-principal at Central High School in Camden. I served in this capacity as long as I was at Camden, which was nine years. During my last year in Camden, I was selected as Benton County Man of the Year.

While at Camden, I served as Home Missions Secretary, working with Brother Gerald Davis who was Home Missions Director for the State of Tennessee, and of course, I worked each summer on "Holiness Hill" in the dining hall, along with several more of my preacher friends.

In 1980, Rev. M. H. Hansford, who was serving as District Secretary of the Tennessee District, United Pentecostal Church, resigned from his office. The brethren of the Tennessee District saw fit to elect me as the next District Secretary-Treasurer. I resigned my position as vice-principal in the Benton County School System and also the pastorate of the First United Pentecostal Church and moved to Jackson, Tennessee to assume my new position which I held for the next 15 years.

During the time that I served as District Secretary, I served as interim pastor at eleven churches in the Tennessee District.

My girls finished their high school work at South Side High School in Jackson, and it wasn't long until Tami got her eye on a young man who had moved to Jackson from

Illinois. His name was Norman Reid. They were married and about five years later my first grandchild arrived, Justin Grant Reid. I will never forget the first time I saw my first grandchild at the hospital. What a great day! Norman had a brother by the name of Tim Reid. It wasn't long before love bloomed, and Sonna and Tim were married! Sisters had married brothers! After a while another grandson came along, James Tyler Reid, son of Sonna and Tim! I couldn't believe I then had two grandsons! Then Norman and Tami had another child, Matthew Wayne Reid. Now I had three grandsons. What a joy they are to my life. A doctor told us that double first cousins are genetically the same as brothers.

All my years of serving as District Secretary were under the leadership of Rev. L. H. Benson. We traveled many miles together and faced several difficult situations together. Due to declining health, Brother Benson decided not to allow his name to run again for Superintendent.

It would not be right to close this chapter without mentioning the impact that Rev. W. M. Greer has had on my life and my ministry. He always believed in me and felt that I could succeed in the ministry. I deeply appreciate his leadership and guidance. He was my friend!

At the District Conference that we held in Memphis, Tennessee in April 1995, the brethren elected me to serve as their Superintendent. Rev. Harold Jaco, Jr. was elected to replace me as District Secretary.

During my tenure as Superintendent, I have served on the Tupelo Children's Mansion board for 19 years and served on the General Board of the United Pentecostal Church for four years.

I suppose the biggest project of my administration is the construction of the new Lake Benson Camp and Christian Retreat Center. We instituted a program called, "Do It

For The Children, which has proven very successful. God has helped us in this endeavor. When the project is finished we will have a campground worth several million dollars.

We do believe the Lord is coming soon. We must work like He is not coming for many years, but live like He's coming today!

My family attends the Lighthouse United Pentecostal Church where Rev. Ron Brown is the pastor. I'm not a very faithful "saint", as I am not there very often due to my travels in the District work, ministering in various churches, etc., but we deeply appreciate them and their arms of love that have been extended to my family.

In closing this autobiography, I want to say that I appreciate my wife who has stood by me in the good times and the bad times; my beautiful daughters, Sonna and Tami, who have been and still are, a continued source of inspiration to me; and my sons-in-law, Norman and Tim Reid; and my grandsons, Justin, Tyler and Matthew, who are the light of my life. I say thanks to all of them. But most of all I thank the Lord Jesus Christ, for without Him, life would be empty and worthless.

Each morning I ask myself, "What can I take credit for in my life?" The answer is, "almost nothing!" Even though I take credit for almost nothing, I can do all things through Christ.

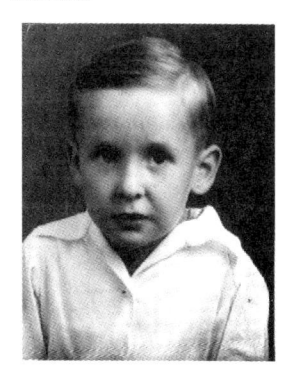

Wayne Chester, age 3. This little boy could have had no idea what the Lord had in store for him in the future.

The Wayne Chester Family. L to R: Carolyn Chester, Wayne Chester, Tim Reid, Sonna Reid, Tami Reid, Norman Reid. Children seated: Justin Reid, Tyler Reid and Matthew Reid.

PROCLAIMING THE YEAR OF JUBILEE
Leviticus 25:11 *"A Jubilee shall that fiftieth year be unto you:"*
Carl McKellar

The Tennessee District of the United Pentecostal Church International held their 50th Anniversary at the Bemis Pentecostal Church the week of April 5 through April 9, 1999. "An Illustrious Past – Illuminates the Future" was the theme of the Jubilee Conference for the entire week of celebration. The Conference returned to the birthplace of the Tennessee District, which was first called the Southern District and was held at the Bemis Pentecostal Church in 1949. During that first Conference, Rev. W. M. Greer was elected by the ministers to be the Superintendent of the newly organized Tennessee District.

The Jubilee Conference began Monday night with a program entitled "Memories of Yesterday, Blessings of Today, Hope for Tomorrow." Rev. Harold Jaco presented a tribute to our present Superintendent Wayne Chester and there was a video presentation with pictures shown from the campground called "Holiness Hill" in Perryville, Tennessee and of the present location at Lake Benson near Dickson,

Tennessee. The service concluded with a great and challenging message from Superintendent Wayne Chester.

Tuesday's service was entitled "Recall, Rejoice, Regroup." Rev. Bob Depriest presented a tribute to Former Superintendent L. H. Benson. A video presentation was shown featuring new churches that have been built throughout the state in the last several years. Brother Benson preached an encouraging and uplifting message. The service ended with an altar service for those who needed a special touch from the Lord.

Everyone who attended the weeklong celebration of Jubilee was anticipating the Wednesday evening service. The theme for the service was "Always Looking Forward" and featured a wonderful tribute by present Superintendent Wayne Chester to Rev. W. M. Greer, District Superintendent-Emeritus. Rev. Paul Price, Superintendent of the California District, presented some great and rare video footage of old-time Pentecost in Tennessee. The service was powerfully blessed when Rev. Greer delivered his message to the congregation stating that he had started walking with the Lord in 1928 and "By the Grace of God, I am still going in that direction." This was Rev. Greer's last message as he went Home to be with the Lord on November 3, 1999. This year of Jubilee for the District became his year of Jubilee forever in the presence of the Lord.

Daytime sessions began on Thursday and Friday. Rev. Harold Jaco, the Secretary-Treasurer of the Tennessee District, spoke in the morning devotion on Thursday. Rev. Jimmy Griggs of Rockwood, Tennessee ministered on Thursday afternoon along with the presentation of the financial and departmental reports. The evening service was a wonderful time of Jubilee honoring those who were being ordained into the ministry. General Superintendent Nathaniel A. Urshan delivered a powerful message challenging the three couples to proclaim the Name of the Lord with full consecration and dedication to the calling of the Lord in their lives.

Friday was a day of generalized business with the election of officers and the presenting of resolutions that were considered by the Conference. The business service was dismissed with great anticipation of greater blessings to come for the Tennessee District. Friday evening service was the annual Youth Rally with outgoing District Youth President Evan Miller, delivering a timely message to the young people of the Tennessee District. He challenged them to follow after the moving of the Holy Spirit and to commit their lives to the Lord for direction and purpose in His Kingdom. Realizing that the Lord has brought us 50 years to this place, only to establish us for the next 50 years, if He tarries. Let us keep the vision for now and beyond. The service ended with a great and wonderful manifestation of the Lord's presence.

The week of Jubilee for the Tennessee District was truly another historical mark upon this great people to continue to do the will of God that His work may be accomplished before His return for His great church. We must celebrate the past to be inspired of what the Lord is still able to do for us as we go into the future with hope and faith of what He is able to perform through us.